## BECOMING A PERSON WHO WALKS WITH GOD

BECOMING A PERSON WHO WALKS WITH GOD

BOBBY PERRY

Unless otherwise indicated, all Scripture quotations in this book marked NKJV are taken from the New King James Version of the Bible. Copyright © 1982 by Thomas Nelson, Inc. Used by permission.

## Just BE!

Copyright © 2012 by **Robert Perry**

Paperback ISBN 978-0-9839613-6-9
eBook ISBN 978-0-9883707-0-8
Library of Congress Control Number 2012949241

Collaborative Development by **Segun Adebayo**

Published by
**GodKulture Publishing**
Chicago, Illinois

Phone: 402-419-1072
Email: publishing@GodKulture.org
www.GodKulturepublishing.com

This publication may not be reproduced, stored in a retrieval system, or transmitted in whole or in part, in any form or by any means, electronic, mechanical, photocopying, recording, or otherwise, without prior written permission of the publisher.

All rights reserved
Printed in United States of America

# *Dedication*

I would like to dedicate this book to my mother, Mrs. Lorene Turner. She has given me the tools and provided the first platform for me to learn and grow in the things of God.

Ma, your sacrifice for my siblings and me was great and your courage is an awesome example of how to *Just BE!* all that God has designed us to be. I hope this book in some small way reflects the sentiments of my experience and my appreciation to you.

# *Appreciation*

I appreciate my immediate family and every member of our church, Kingdom Builders' Worship Center. We have taken this journey of *Just BE!* together.

It's my prayer that the revelation contained in this book would be life changing and would continue to help you to build the Kingdom of God on earth as it is in heaven.

# Contents

|   |   |   |
|---|---|---|
|   | Prologue | 9 |
| 1 | *Belonging* to God's Family | 11 |
| 2 | *Believing* Him | 29 |
| 3 | Leaving the Past *Behind* | 47 |
| 4 | *Beginning* a New Walk | 63 |
| 5 | *Beseeching* Him | 81 |
| 6 | *Behaving* Like Christ | 99 |
|   | Epilogue | 119 |
|   | Believer's Meditation | 121 |
|   | A New Life | 127 |

# *Prologue*

To ***be*** or not to ***be*** is far more than a question. It's actually a mandate from God that we must ***be*** all that He desires for us. When God created everything, He spoke it into existence by saying a powerful prophetic phrase "Let There BE…" Whatever followed "Let There BE" manifested in the earth simply by the desire and design of God's creative thinking.

God said Let There BE light and then light shined through the darkness. This is an example of God's sovereign authority in the earth. In this, we discover His will for us. He wants us to have the same creative thinking and mirror His desire for things to *Just BE*. We must speak things into our atmosphere by faith and watch it come to pass.

The Gospel message is the good news of Jesus Christ and it addresses our need to *belong* to something and someone greater than ourselves. This message also challenges and changes what we *believe*. As we continue studying the Gospel and applying its principles to our lives, it will impact how we *behave* which ultimately produces what we will *become*.

It's every believer's goal to be more like Christ. In order to do this, we need to know Him through the power of His resurrection and also through the fellowship of His sufferings. This however takes a great deal of sacrifice on our part. Paul, the Apostle gives us an example of the measure of this sacrifice when he says, I've been crucified with Christ; nevertheless I live. Yet not I, but Christ lives within me. He says that the life that he lives now, he lives by faith in the Son of God. Our entire lives must be built on faith.

In *Just BE!* It's my goal to reveal a process to becoming a person who walks with God. Walking with God is not just a Sunday morning journey but it's a daily encounter through a lifestyle of fellowship with Him. Our position in Christ must have a strong foundation of faith in His Word. To that end, I have provided scriptures on Pages 121-125 to help strengthen your faith.

The Bible says that faith comes by hearing and hearing by the word of God. As you embark on this journey with me through the pages of *Just BE!* I want to saturate your heart and your atmosphere with so much of the Word of God that your entire life would reflect the riches of His glory.

It's my prayer that you enjoy reading this book and more importantly that the revelation contained therein will help you to *Just BE!*"

**Bobby Perry**
**Boston, Massachusetts**

# Chapter 1
## BELONGING TO GOD'S FAMILY

*Not forsaking the assembling of ourselves together, as is the manner of some, but exhorting one another, and so much the more as you see the Day approaching.*
**(Hebrews 10:25)**

## In this Chapter, you will learn about:

- ➢ What is Fellowship?
- ➢ Loving Others
- ➢ Benefits of Fellowship
- ➢ A Prevailing Church

## WHAT IS FELLOWSHIP?

> *And they continued steadfastly in the apostles' doctrine and fellowship, in the breaking of bread, and in prayers.*
> **Acts 2:42**

One of the four things the early church devoted itself to was "fellowship." Fellowship was a very important part of their reason for meeting together. It was one of their objectives. But what is fellowship? Fellowship is defined as companionship or a group of people coming together to share common interest, activity, or experience. Among Christians, the common bond is their faith in Christ.

The Greek word for fellowship is *Koinonia*, meaning communion, fellowship, and participation with Christ in His sufferings, in the gifts and grace of the Holy Spirit in this life and in the glories of the next life. We often hear people talking about fellowship but our modern ideas of fellowship have become so watered down that the word no longer carries the same meaning it did in New Testament times.

We are not surprised by the fruitfulness of the early church because it devoted itself to "the apostles' teaching" and also "to prayer." Apart from the ministry of the Holy Spirit, these are the two most important means of growth, power, and effectiveness in the Christian life and this is evident everywhere in the rest of scripture.

Apostle Luke, who wrote the book of Acts, stated that these early Christians also devoted themselves to fellowship. They didn't just *have* fellowship, they *devoted* themselves to it because it was a priority for them. It is not just about coming together, but fellowship with Christ and His suffering, sharing with one another in love. In view of this, the Bible says:

> *Not forsaking the assembling of ourselves together, as is the manner of some, but exhorting one another, and so much the more as you see the Day approaching.*
> **Hebrews 10:25**

The Bible instructs us not to forsake going to regular meetings with other believers, yet others, who may have become fed up with church, seek fellowship through viewing a worship service on television, but this too misses the point. Joel S. McCraw, the retired senior pastor of Faith Chapel in Huntsville, Alabama, once suggested that "If you are one of those who gets their religion by watching religious broadcasts on television, or listening to the gospel via radio, you might want to step up to the set after a service and "Give your TV a great big hug."

The early church came together not only for spiritual enrichment but also for social enhancement through practical conversations. This was only possible because they genuinely loved one another. In this present dispensation, we worship and pray with one another, we give our tithes and offerings for the advancement of the fellowship, but we fall short of speaking and encouraging one another.

As believers, it is imperative that we extend the hand of love to our fellow brethren. We cannot love others in our human strength but only through the work of the Holy Spirit in us. We might have had some ill experience with some believers in the past that could make it hard to love but it is for our own good that we present ourselves as a living sacrifice to God so that He can remove the heart of stone from us and give us a heart of flesh to love like Him.

The electronic religion of multitudes of people creates emptiness, thus interpersonal relationships are so desperately needed to keep our faith glowing and growing. If you dissociate yourself from other Christians in worship and service, you'll run out of spiritual fervor and dedication in a short time. There is no substitute for going to church and worshiping with others of like precious faith.

You may be thinking that your view of fellowship is much richer and deeper than mere social activity. True fellowship involves getting together not only for prayer and discussing God's Word, but also for using the Word to encourage, comfort, and edify one another. And you are right. This certainly is an aspect of Christian fellowship that is often lacking in the church today and it needs to be reestablished.

There are two forms of fellowship, which are *vertical and horizontal dimensions*. The first one is our communion with our Lord Jesus Christ through worship, prayer, and the meditation on His Word. The language of God's kingdom is love, and to effortlessly express this language, we need to be in union with God, for God is love. The more we meditate on love, the more we empower our will to love.

When we love as God loves, His light shines on us to see as He sees so that we can practice the truths we read and hear. Jesus' resurrection power is available for us as believers but there is a price to pay in fellowshipping in His suffering, by dying to self so that we can be a partaker of His glory.

The second dimension has to do with our fellowship with other believers. As we grow in the knowledge of God, it will be easier to converse with other Christians.

This heart to heart talk is very essential because it is through that we can know why some say what they say or act the way they act. Speaking in tongues for over two hours is wonderful but of what benefit is it if we cannot talk with our brethren in English for a few minutes.

> *Can two walk together, unless they are agreed?*
> **Amos 3:3**

We need to be together in fellowship so that there will be no division. We cannot be tied together with people we are not in agreement with. Walking in love with our fellow believers depend on how much of God's nature have been imparted on us through communion with Him. We should be more concerned with the interest of others than ours while coming together in fellowship. As a member of the body of Christ, this should be our focus, so that unity can be fostered.

## LOVING OTHERS

> *That He would grant you, according to the riches of His glory, to be strengthened with might through His Spirit in the inner man, $^{17}$that Christ may dwell in your hearts through faith; that you, being rooted and grounded in love, $^{18}$may be able to comprehend with all the saints what is the width and length and depth and height— $^{19}$to know the love of Christ which passes knowledge; that you may be filled with all the fullness of God.*
> **Ephesians 3:16-19**

For us to have a thriving fellowship, it is necessary that we understand the depth of God's love for us, so as to be able to see through His eyes and heart. All our ability to love has been limited by our experiences in this life. Until and unless we break free from our own experiential limitations, we will never be able to fully comprehend God's love. God is the Father and Creator of all life, all souls and all spirit beings. There is a tenderness that one has when one is the source and creator of life.

A tiny, tiny measure is seen in the sacrificial love that parents have for their children. In the eyes of many mothers, if the most evil criminal were their own son, he would still have some qualities worth redeeming. The ability of parents and lovers to see good in the object of their love is beyond comprehension. In the eyes of God, every human soul has good qualities and beauty yet unlocked.

For God has seen the end of all evil in our future and thus dares to allow evil to exist alongside good. We humans find it difficult to keep a loving attitude towards the most hideous of human monsters that show evil in their lives especially when they destroy millions of others. Yet God alone can see some good there that He still would have sent His son if they were the only ones left in the world.

God loved us while we were yet sinners. We were not just sinners; we were enemies in the sight of God. We were evil and sinners in His sight, yet He loved us! Many of us cannot understand this unconditional love of God in the same way that Prophet Jonah did not understand God's love and mercy. The Assyrians were the most wicked and evil of all the people who had conquered Jerusalem.

Some of their deeds according to historians were the skinning of people while still alive, killing babies and children, pregnant women pierced alive with the sword, and various other methods of evil and torture that are not even imaginable in our modern days. Their wickedness came right up to the throne of God (Jonah 1:2).

Yet God sent Jonah to warn them and when they responded to Jonah's preaching and repented, God forgave them. Jonah hated them so much that he did not take delight in God pardoning them and God had to teach Jonah a lesson through a plant. Many of us would have been displeased with God and even angry like Jonah was. This is how we feel towards all those evil people in our recent history. Jonah would rather die than see them forgiven by God (Jonah 4).

> *Judge not, that you be not judged. ²For with what judgment you judge, you will be judged; and with the measure you use, it will be measured back to you. ³And why do you look at the speck in your brother's eye, but do not consider the plank in your own eye?*
> **Matthew 7:1-3**

Many Christians feel what they call righteous indignation so much that some extreme ones have even advocated taking the law into their own hands. I do realize that this imperfect planet needs the law and a system of good government that deals severely with lawlessness in proportion to its wickedness.

It is only right that for society and civilization to exist and grow to its height, the evil and the lawless must be dealt with and put away. However, there is a big difference between God meting out judgment and humans judging.

With God His anger is only on the surface to show His displeasure but His heart is always full of love. For everyone makes judgments in life and situations in order to make the right decisions, but only God has the right to judge people eternally. Our attribute should always be love, love and love.

We must raise our ability to love to the level of God. We must acquire the ability to see beauty where all is ashes, to see good where all is evil, to see love where all is hate. Only then can we love as God loves. Also what we are able to see is limited by who we are. A covetous person will notice others who are covetous. A greedy person will see greed in others. A proud person will see only pride in others.

What we notice most in others are the things that we secretly treasure in our selves. What we like in ourselves are also what we like in others. Our very ability to love and relate to others is equal to the same ability that we have relating to ourselves. We are limited by our very own selves and not by God. Thus we must cast aside all these limitations and take on the limitless quality of the Spirit of God.

> *And this I pray, that your love may abound still more and more in knowledge and all discernment, [10]that you may approve the things that are excellent, that you may be sincere and without offense till the day of Christ, [11]being filled with the fruits of righteousness which are by Jesus Christ, to the glory and praise of God.*
> **Philippians 1:9-11**

How can we be perfect and loving like God unless we also find the power of love within us even when we are drowned with raw emotions of hate towards sin and wickedness?

Never ever let the sin, evil and imperfection in others around you rob you of the ability to keep a loving attitude towards them. Instead let love always be your default attribute. Then will we be perfect like our Heavenly Father is perfect.

It is imperative that we seek to find good where there is only evil, love where there is only hatred and joy where there is only pain and suffering. The day we can discover these, then are we on our way to becoming more like God. Look for beauty in others and you will see it and feel the love that God feels for them. Every soul who has come to this earth is lovely in the sight of God.

God still feels connected to each soul in the same way that we feel connected to our physical body. We would not cut off our own hands or our own legs, thus God would not cut off His love to any of His creation no matter how imperfect they seem to be. Let us feel and see this unconditional love that God perpetually has with His own creation as we come together in fellowship.

## BENEFITS OF FELLOWSHIP

> *From whom the whole body, joined and knit together by what every joint supplies, according to the effective working by which every part does its share, causes growth of the body for the edifying of itself in love.*
> **Ephesians 4:16**

Having established the concept of fellowship and the dynamics of loving others, we now want to expound on the advantages of fellowship.

It is important to be in a fruitful fellowship and not just be a successful member of a fellowship. God has ordained that we all function as parts within the body of Christ and not the whole body in ourselves. Of course, each part of the body of Christ must discover its own function to be successful in contributing to the whole body. Every member has something to contribute as we assemble together in love.

## (1) Covering of Blind Spots

We all have blind spots because of the way our eyes function in looking forward. Our peripheral vision has areas in which we need mirrors in the car to cover when we drive. Also, we are all taught in good driving to turn and check our blind spots whenever we change lanes. Those are physical blind spots. Soul and spiritual blind spots are harder to find because people don't know how to turn their soul around and look at their soul's blind spots.

We don't see what we can't see. We are unaware of what we have no knowledge of. Only as we relate and fellowship with others can we be aware of how different we are from others. Jacob had a blind spot for his son Joseph, loving him above all the other sons. He was not very much like God our Father who loves all of us equally in Christ. Part of the reason for the strife in his own family was his own fault of unfairly favoring Joseph above all his other sons.

Joseph made it worse by his own bad report of his brothers to his father. All these worsening situations headed for a major crisis, which Jacob suffered years of grief that he never recovered from. It is amazing to see God working His plans through such a plethora of human imperfection.

However, we can never excuse the human responsibilities which caused grief and suffering to all concerned (Genesis 37). If only Jacob had someone to tell him that he was doing wrong by favoring one son above eleven others, the grief he experienced would have been lessened, and God would still have fulfilled His plan.

For us to have effective fellowship, we should be eyes for those without eyes and legs for those without legs, so that our inadequacy can be catered for. Iron sharpens iron and the wounds of a friend are better than the kisses of an enemy.

## (2) Complementing Our Individual Limitations

> *And the eye cannot say to the hand, "I have no need of you"; nor again the head to the feet, "I have no need of you." $^{22}$No, much rather, those members of the body which seem to be weaker are necessary.*
> **1 Corinthians 12:21-22**

The apostle Paul and Barnabas are two contrasting personalities and individuals. Paul was an intellectual who reasoned and debated but Barnabas was an encourager who stood up for those who were outcasts. Barnabas was instrumental in standing up for Paul when no one wanted to be with him after his conversion.

It was this same characteristic that made him stand up for Mark when Paul did not want Mark to follow them after Mark's earlier desertion. In this particular incident, Barnabas was right and Paul was wrong. We are all growing in the things of God all the time. We can all aim for perfection but not all of us are there yet.

In the light of these matters, we should be willing to fellowship with other believers so that we can learn from one another. No one person knows everything. Since God does not speak in English but speaks Spirit to spirit within us, even our understanding of what He is saying is subjective to our translation and interpretation.

When we claim that we have been in the light and have been hearing and walking in God, we will delight in joining with others who have been in the light. The fire burns brighter when all the flames gather together than to be scattered in individual flames.

## (3) Ability Enhancement

This has to do with the ability to exert greater than normal individual capability. For instance, David brought together men of similar gifts which strengthened their respective giftings. Those who were warriors when gathered together became the mighty men of David, spurring one another to acts of bravery. The skilled musicians gathered together by David to serve God in the tabernacle impelled a whole generation of musicians and worshippers that continued through Solomon's time.

> *Again I say to you that if two of you agree on earth concerning anything that they ask, it will be done for them by My Father in heaven. [20]For where two or three are gathered together in My name, I am there in the midst of them.*
> **Matthew 18:19-20**

The promises of Jesus have always involved the release of a team ministry (fellowship). I believe that this promise has yet to be fully tapped.

Many relationships between good Christian friends have a potential to reach this powerful level, where, one can chase a thousand, two chase ten thousand, three chase a hundred thousand and four a million.

No one reaches his full stature without linking up with the right people in fellowship. Even Daniel had his three friends that helped him reach the pinnacle of the world's greatest empire in God's sight. Think about those whom God has sent to be with you, to stand with you and to link up spiritually with you to change the world.

Sometimes we reject them because they are not like us but you will find the common bond in that each would love God with all their heart, mind, soul and strength. It doesn't matter how different others are. It only matters that they love the same God. When the church has reached its *oneness* in God, the world will see the greatest manifestation of the glory of God (John 17:22).

## A PREVAILING CHURCH

> *Simon Peter answered and said, "You are the Christ, the Son of the living God." [17]Jesus answered and said to him, "Blessed are you, Simon Bar-Jonah, for flesh and blood has not revealed this to you, but My Father who is in heaven. [18]And I also say to you that you are Peter, and on this rock I will build **My church**, and the gates of Hades shall not **prevail** against it. [19]And I will give you the keys of the kingdom of heaven, and whatever you bind on earth will be bound in heaven, and whatever you loose on earth will be loosed in heaven."*
> **Matthew 16:16-19**

There are churches that are named after places and people, but they can never claim origin or ownership, because Christ owns the church. Jesus told Simon Peter: *"You are Peter, and on this rock I will build my church."* The church is built on the revelation of who Christ is and the Kingdom is established through demonstration of what we know.

Could it be that there is very little Kingdom demonstration in the earth because there is very little church revelation? Jesus is concerned about building His church! We have the responsibility of managing what He builds and building what He will manage.

The Greek word for church is *ekklesia*, meaning being called out of this world of humanity to form a body of believers in *fellowship* that belongs exclusively to Jesus.

The word *prevail* means to prove more powerful than an opposing force or be victorious. The church of Jesus Christ is not to conform to its environment but to *prevail* against any contrary circumstances because it is meant to be a light to those in darkness. A prevailing church is a fruitful growing *fellowship* that is *extending* a hand of love to *the world* around them, because it is not only to be in the four corners of a building.

The church needs to know its purpose in order to be successful in its mission. The church exists to manifest the *presence* of God to *everyone* around them, so that through it, *they* can see them as a *portrait* of God's Kingdom. As people who were once in darkness embrace the kingdom lifestyle, they experience the *power* of God.

The three purposes (presence, portrait, power) of the church are expounded below.

## (1) Presence

> *You are the light of the world. A city that is set on a hill cannot be hidden. <sup>15</sup>Nor do they light a lamp and put it under a basket, but on a lampstand, and it gives light to all who are in the house. <sup>16</sup>Let your light so shine before men, that they may see your good works and glorify your Father in heaven.*
> **Matthew 5:14-16**

So what would a church have to do with the demonstration of God's presence? Its people would have to live like Him! Characterized by hospitality, the loving acceptance of all kinds of people, a quickness to serve, a tangible love for one another that makes people feel secure, and a patient tolerance of one another's weaknesses would all be a great way to start. Paul said we should walk in a manner, *"worthy of the Lord"* (Colossians 1:10). Let's live in such a way that others will experience the presence of the God who lives in us, wherever we are, but especially at church.

## (2) Portrait

> *Beloved, now we are children of God; and it has not yet been revealed what we shall be, but we know that when He is revealed, we shall be like Him, for we shall see Him as He is.*
> **1 John 3:2**

The vision Jesus gave His church in His Word is a Christ centered revelation or insight to prepare His body for His return. The vision should never be to promote man or a human agenda. Every Christ centered church should have a vision that promotes the Kingdom Agenda. What is that?

It is the plan to build the domain of the King. Jesus Christ is the King of kings, with each citizen of the kingdom as kings, living a kingdom lifestyle.

### (3) Power

As stated in Matthew 16:16-19 above, God has given us a mission to change the landscape of our world. To do that there must be *prevailing* power. We can go confidently into the world with the message of the gospel, knowing that the power of the resurrected Christ goes with us, and that there is no one who is so trapped by the power of the devil that the power of the gospel cannot set free. Everywhere the gospel is preached the church triumphs over evil, the kingdom expands and evil retreats.

## Kingdom Keys

(1) Our coming together in fellowship should not only be for *spiritual* enrichment but also for *social* enhancement through practical conversations.

(2) The *language* of God's kingdom is *love*, and to effortlessly express this language, we need to be in union with God, so as to be able to see through His eyes and heart.

(3) Our very ability to love and *relate* to others is equal to the same ability that we have *relating* to ourselves. We are *limited* by our very own selves and not by God.

(4) For us to have *effective* fellowship, we should be eyes for those without eyes and legs for those without legs, so that our *inadequacy* can be catered for.

(5) When the church has reached its *oneness* in God, the world will see the greatest manifestation of the *glory* of God (John 17:22).

(6) The church of Jesus Christ is not to *conform* to its environment but to *prevail* against any contrary circumstances because it is meant to be a light to those in darkness.

(7) A prevailing church is a fruitful growing *fellowship* that is *extending* a hand of love to the *world* around them, because it is not only to be in the four corners of a building.

(8) The church is built on revelation or knowledge of who Christ is. His Kingdom is established in the earth through demonstration of what has been revealed.

# Chapter 2
## BELIEVING HIM

*By faith we understand that the worlds were framed by the word of God, so that the things which are seen were not made of things which are visible. ⁶But without faith it is impossible to please Him, for he who comes to God must believe that He is, and that He is a rewarder of those who diligently seek Him.*
**(Hebrews 11:3, 6)**

## In this Chapter, you will learn about:

- ➢ The Importance of The Word
- ➢ The Process of Faith
- ➢ How Faith Sees
- ➢ The Work of Faith

## THE IMPORTANCE OF THE WORD

The Church is not a social organization, even though it has communal programs, but it is a group of people with the life of God coming together to influence the world. Many people are in bondage to the god of this world, and to be an instrument of deliverance to these multitudes, we need to believe God to do the impossible. This requires we develop uncommon faith in Him. Faith comes by reading and hearing the Word of God and meditating on it.

> *In the beginning was the Word, and the Word was with God, and the Word was God. ²He was in the beginning with God. ³All things were made through Him, and without Him nothing was made that was made. ⁴In Him was life, and the life was the light of men. ⁵And the light shines in the darkness, and the darkness did not comprehend it.*
> **John 1:1-4**

God's Word holds a central place in all of His dealings with us. Jesus did many wonderful works and signs while on earth but in His prayer in John 17, He was most concerned about the keeping of His words and teachings, which He left with the disciples (John 17:6-8). If we abandon His Word, we abandon the only weapon we have (the sword of the Spirit) against the forces of darkness.

The true work of the Holy Spirit is to confirm (not replace) the Word of God with signs following. Some may protest that the Word preached in many churches is dry and stale but this is not because of the Word, rather it is the lack of it, which has been replaced with man's traditions and customs.

The Word of God delivered by the unction of the Holy Spirit can never be stale. Some have neglected the Word for the Spirit in their enthusiasm to be part of the latest move of God and went into extreme errors. We should not just be content with the demonstrations of the Spirit nor be satisfied with the teaching of the Word; but be zealous for both.

A friend once said, "the Word without the Spirit would make one *dry up*; the Spirit without the Word would make one *blow up*; but the Word and the Spirit together would help one to *grow up*!" Those who hear the voice of the Spirit and yield to both the new move of the Word and the Spirit will perform great exploits in these last days.

Since our concern is for God's Kingdom to be established on earth, we can learn from the early church, which took their world for Jesus, by preaching the unadulterated Word of God. The revival in the book of Acts was a revival of both the Word and the Spirit. In Acts 1, the disciples obeyed the Word of the Lord by staying in Jerusalem to continually pray for the Spirit.

According to Acts 2, three thousand souls were saved when the Holy Spirit came down after the Word was preached. The Spirit confirmed the Word with signs and wonders. The Word grew and spread after the appointment of the seven deacons because the apostles wanted to devote more time to the Word and prayer. The Kingdom of God expanded rapidly when they took the Word seriously (Acts 6).

Our Lord Jesus was the Word made flesh and He was anointed with the Spirit without measure. Let us be the generation that will tap into the fullest manifestation and allow the Word and the Spirit to flow through our lives until we are fully transformed to Christ likeness, then the church will be ready for Jesus at His coming. When the Word is infused into our lives, our *belief level* is increased. How does this work?

## THE PROCESS OF FAITH

Union with Christ is the beginning, the middle and the end of all of our Christian life. When we are born again, we begin the process of discipleship with Christ (He's in us). As we grow, we begin to see the benefits of discipleship (life in Him) and as we mature in later years, we begin to see the greater fullness of us being in Him.

Much has been taught about faith in Christendom but we need to understand clearly, in summary, the whole process of faith taking place. Thus, every Christian must be able to understand and outline the ABCs of faith at all times just like a kindergarten child should be able to recite his ABCs and 123s. In teaching people God's kind of faith, we need to emphasize that faith does grow.

In essence, the beginning of faith is the discovery of what God has promised us through Christ and the reception of which produces the same faith that helps us to lay hold of what Christ has done for us. Faith goes through its typical cycle of hearing, believing, receiving, acting and final manifestation of the object of faith.

In the process, we are transformed. Once we receive the word of faith specifically for our lives, we must allow the process of faith to take place within us.

What Jesus authored within us through His Word needs to be nurtured in the fertile ground of our lives for it to grow.

> *As it is written, "I have made you a father of many nations" in the presence of Him whom he believed—God, who gives life to the dead and calls those things which do not exist as though they did; $^{18}$who, contrary to hope, in hope believed, so that he became the father of many nations, according to what was spoken, "So shall your descendants be." $^{19}$And not being weak in faith, he did not consider his own body, already dead since he was about a hundred years old, and the deadness of Sarah's womb. $^{20}$He did not waver at the promise of God through unbelief, but was strengthened in faith, giving glory to God. $^{21}$and being fully convinced that what He had promised He was also able to perform.*
> **Romans 4:17-21**

The life of Abraham, who is the father of faith, outlines the process of four stages (Visualization, Nurturing, Praising and Conviction) for us as follows:

**(1) Visualization Stage:** Abraham believed beyond natural hope. To achieve this process, God had him visualizing the sand and the stars as His children (Genesis 13; 15). God asked him to 'walk through the length and breadth of the physical land' specifically telling him to lift up his eyes and see. God specifically ushered Abraham outside of his tent to look up at the stars and see them as his children. This special emphasis teaches the great importance of visualization in the beginning of faith. Visualization is the key to allowing the growth and strengthening of faith within us.

**(2) Nurturing Stage:** Abraham was *not* weak in faith by *not* considering his infertile body nor the deadness of Sarah's womb. There are some things we should do and there are some things which we should not do. The best way to nurture the growth of our faith is to look beyond all natural impossibilities. Faith is the key spiritual instrument to work in the impossible realm, if we keep considering the impossibilities of the natural limiting laws, we will never have the faith to move into the realm of the impossible.

**(3) Praising Stage:** As we receive the promise of God's Word, we need *not* to waver; instead, we need to be strengthened in faith, by giving glory to God. This means the constant thanksgiving and praise and worship of faith being offered up to God. There are, of course, varying levels of conviction and assurances but we are to allow this growth process of visualization and thanksgiving daily until we reach the full assurance of faith. It is a process within a process, and one should not be impatient but allow the Word, the blood and the Spirit to work within us for the inward transformation which effects the outward manifestation.

**(4) Conviction Stage:** Finally Abraham was fully convinced that what God had promised, He would also perform. Yet, Abraham did falter when he had Ishmael and also when he first laughed in unbelief. How can this be possible, we might say? Well, as long as there is a soul and a spirit part within us, there is always a possibility of the spirit part believing while the soul part is still in unbelief and doubt. For that reason, the possibility of double-mindedness is a reality. There is an inner knowing and conviction that arises out of our spirit which is different from the knowing and conviction of the soul mind.

All we need to do is to know that the constant and daily process of meditation on God's Word, visualization, thanksgiving with praise and worship to God causes a strengthening of the spirit man such that the soul mind will begin to be in harmony with the mind of the spirit.

In the depths beyond consciousness (subconscious), the Word of God is separating our soul mind from the spirit mind, purifying, renewing, establishing, discerning, sharpening and strengthening in ways beyond our understanding like the way the marrow in our bones produces life giving blood cells (Hebrews 4:12). We don't have to do too much thinking and rationalization but we do have to allow all the processes of faith to take place within us and in time, the fullness of the assurance and conviction of faith will take place naturally.

The above is a summary of the process of faith that should help us to know what is taking place from the very first time that the seed of faith comes into our heart through a personal word from the Lord. Growing spiritually and making progress in our walk with God, demands that we give attention to the Word we receive in meditation, visualization, in confession, in thanksgiving, praise and worship. There is no easy road to glory, the choice is yours!

## HOW FAITH SEES

> *Blessed are the pure in heart, for they shall see God.*
> **Matthew 5:8**

In focusing on the visualizing aspect of the walk of faith, many who are still substantiating the things hoped for into manifestation by faith, still do not have a clear vision or picture of what the end result of faith looks like.

There is no such thing as one self-authoring their faith. Faith comes from Jesus and Jesus alone. It is for this reason that one looks to Jesus both from the beginning of faith to the completion of faith.

Therefore, before anyone launches into the prayer of faith, the first thing that must be done is to be in union with Jesus experientially to receive the specific authoring and initiation of faith for the object of prayer. Without taking this first step, many people exercise their own human confidence or presumption in believing, confessing or visualizing that, which could have been born out of their own flesh and soul.

The human soul has an ability to imitate those same areas of the human spirit but to no avail and zero results. The best position to be in is to behold Jesus, be in love with Jesus, be enamored by His love and presence. How do we know that we are experiencing this love? When we begin to love God with all our heart, mind, soul and strength!

However, many only superficially experience that and know it in their heads but not in their hearts. The reception of God's love is still not sufficient until that same love of God for us causes us to love Him in the same unconditional manner in which He loves us.

> *That Christ may dwell in your hearts through faith; that you, being rooted and grounded in love, $^{18}$may be able to comprehend with all the saints what is the width and length and depth and height— $^{19}$to know the love of Christ which passes knowledge; that you may be filled with all the fullness of God.*
> **Ephesians 3:17-19**

Many people want God to love them unconditionally but they never love Him back the same way.

They will only love Him when things go outwardly well, otherwise, they won't love Him. Such attitudes are childish ways of relating to our God, the creator of the Universe. Job went through trials because God wanted to know his heart as to whether he loved what He could do for him or that he truly loved Him.

God wants us to grow up and not only love Him for what He can do but for who He is. For this reason, sometimes non-charismatics who do not believe in miracles have a steady walk with God despite their belief that the era of miracles have passed away. They have chosen to follow Jesus because of the one act He did for them on the cross, and they ask for nothing more.

Until we understand that our love for Jesus should be unconditional, we will never enter into the sweet fellowship that is reserved for those who love Him without reservation. Of course, God will answer every prayer and keep every promise but even if He does not, will you still love Him? Let us so choose to be in a covenant love relationship with Him. Let us choose to love Him with all of our being.

Once we have beheld Jesus in all His love and glory, then we can yield our hearts for Him to author the vision and picture of all that He wants to do in our lives. We then visualize 'from Him' as He gives us the correct pictures and images for that which is to come. As we daily come into His presence and yield our hearts to Him, the image of the answers to all our desires become painted and completed in vision form.

This is a gradual process, however, for some things it could be at lightning speed while in others it might take years. It is not so much us trying to visualize as it is more the Holy

Spirit painting the detailed picture in our hearts and in the eyes of our spirit. Our eyes of faith in those areas where faith is being exercised becomes sharp like the eagle and we can see the reality of the inner vision before any signs of the physical manifestation takes place.

We become those who see the reality of the invisible while others have yet to see. At first we carry the vision but soon the vision carries us; we live and breathe the vision like Noah building the ark each day. In the exercise of faith, the eyes of faith must be developed to that of an eagle's eye. Those with chicken eyes can never see what only the eagle can see. Like baby eaglets, we should never be discouraged but always do the following in our faith walk:

**(1) Make a Covenant with God:** We make a spiritual agreement with God to love Him unconditionally as much as He has loved us unconditionally. Even if we live and die without seeing one more answer to prayer, we will still love Him with all our heart, mind, soul and strength. Once this consecration of love has taken place in our inner heart, a new strength and steadfastness will be ours for life for we are now established upon the rock of His love. He loves us and we love Him, both being in the eternally unbroken union of God's love (Ephesians 3:17-21).

**(2) Yield our Life to God as a Living Sacrifice:** We should be willing to do all of His will for the rest of our lives. He will begin to author His desires in us and His hand will begin to write in our heart the works that He has predestined for us to do (Ephesians 2:10). The works that He desires for us to walk in will be, through time with Him, written and shown in clarity which we will easily be able to see with the new eyes of faith He gives us. He desires to show great things to those who love Him wholeheartedly.

**(3) Daily Exercise our Eyes of Faith:** With those eyes, we see the completed picture of that which God is doing through us. Visualize the invisible realities before they are manifested in the physical (2 Corinthians 4:18). Exercise with patience and allow the invisible to grow through its full pregnancy before it gives birth in the physical realm. It is my prayer that God would cause the eyes of your understanding to see the wonderful things He has in store for you.

Make this confession with me:
**If I can think it in my mind and believe it in my heart, it will be conceived in my spirit and then birthed into reality!**

## THE WORK OF FAITH

> *Remembering without ceasing your **work of faith**, and labor of love, and patience of hope in our Lord Jesus Christ, in the sight of God and our Father.*
> **1 Thessalonians 1:3 (KJV)**

It is well understood by now that faith is a rest but one also needs to understand the parallel concept of how the work of faith works. The work of faith is the small part or act that is required of us to release and demonstrate our faith. Every miracle of faith recorded in the Bible involved an act that is part of the release of the spiritual energy of faith.

According to the book of Exodus, Moses had to release his faith through the use of the rod before the miracle happened. In the methodology used by Jesus for His miracles in the gospels, there are records of Him using the laying on of hands and other methods like spittle and clay to heal a blind man but the most important common denominator is the use of the spoken word.

The key to understand the act or work of faith is to understand when to act. There is such a thing as the fullness of faith or being full of faith. There are different stages before the ripeness or fullness of time to act on the faith. Different areas and faith expectations will take different time lengths to bring the result of faith into manifestation. Some things take longer than others to birth forth in faith.

In the pregnancy period of faith, the object of faith is not just energized by needs but rather it is energized by God wanting to do something through us. This means that one needs to actually hear God, either through His written Word or His spoken Word for faith to materialize in our spirits. Hearing the voice of God will resonate to our souls as thoughts, impressions, or desires.

The problem is to differentiate between our own thoughts or impressions from those that are reflected by our soul from our spirit man encounter with the Holy Spirit. For this reason, many Christians who have yet to learn to hear God find it difficult to exercise faith as they are not sensitive to yielding and hearing their own spirit man much less the Holy Spirit Himself.

Once the seed of faith is placed into our spirits, the desire, vision or burden for the final manifestation of the ultimate result of faith begins to take place.

Like the seed of God's Word in the parable of the sower and the seed (Mark 4), there are three different tests and temptations that it goes through: the test of doubt and unbelief, the test of persecution and rejection, and the test of ease and worldliness.

Most of the time, God's plan for His people are thwarted through their unbelief, their lack of stamina to go through difficult times of persecution or the distraction of the pleasures of this worldly life. For this reason, there are not many achievements of the acts of faith amongst God's people and the few that succeed are made into heroes of faith when in the New Testament every believer has the potential to be a hero of faith within the circle of their own life.

It is only those who are diligent in nurturing this seed within themselves that receive the end reward. When a believer has passed the above three tests and is fully assured of what God has spoken into their lives, they must then learn to enter the holding pattern of faith and with patience hold on to the seed until it reaches its full pregnancy term and is birthed forth.

> *That you do not become sluggish, but imitate those who through faith and patience inherit the promises.*
> **Hebrews 6:12**

This takes time and only those who mixed their faith with patience will receive the manifestation of faith. Some things take a short time (a few weeks to a few months) but other things take years and even decades. Abraham took about twenty years of walking by faith to bring about the manifestation of his physical promised child.

When the fullness of faith has come, the skill of the birthing process is also important. There are various laws in which one must function in:

**(1) Right Methods:** The methodology will be in line with the anointing or method of releasing one's faith that God has specifically commanded them; for example, Moses using the rod to part the red sea, and Jesus spitting on the eyes of the blind man to heal him.

**(2) Timing:** It is also God who chooses the exact time, the exact place and the exact environment in which the full manifestation of His Word will take place. For instance, when the fullness of time came, God sent His Son, born of woman, to redeem mankind from their sins.

**(3) Harmonization:** It is always a coordinated process in which both the natural world and the spiritual world have worked together to bring about the events (Luke 1; 2). Of course, the faith event of one's personal lives in believing God for the salvation of a loved one might not receive the Hallelujah chorus of the birth of Jesus on earth but every single walk of faith is of great importance to the overall progress of humanity.

**(4) Consistency:** There will always be a key man or woman in whom the seed of faith for that event has been planted. They would have consistently walked in their holding pattern of faith against all odds and still remained standing to bring about the final act of faith, which breaks into the natural world as a demonstration of the faithfulness of God.

**(5) Good Stewardship:** Some acts of faith that have given birth to some events create a great tidal wave immediately but others start with a whisper that results in a tidal wave through time. Each of our lives and walk of faith is important to God. It contributes to the overall progress of humanity towards Him. As He has given us grace to minister as good stewards, we should never seek public attention in our act of faith but always do it as unto the Lord alone to whom we all give an account.

Although David slew Goliath when he went to take lunch for his brothers, he had already, quietly and unseen by public, slain the lion and the bear. Great earth changing events are always a combination of those whose destinies are to change the world and those men and women working in the background or shadows holding the hands of those whom they are chosen to help.

Many people like to be number one but it is just as glorious to be number two or three in the sight of God. We are all to walk in the works that have been created for each of us before the foundation of the earth (Ephesians 2:10). For every leader is only as good as the quality of their followers. Remember that each one of us has an important role to play on earth. Be faithful and be diligent to carry out every command of God, big or small.

## Kingdom Keys

(1) Those who *hear* the voice of the Spirit and yield to both the new move of the Word and the Spirit will *perform* great exploits in these last days.

(2) As we *grow* in our walk with God, we begin to *see* the benefits of the union of life in Him, and as we mature in later years, we begin to *see* the greater fullness of us being in Him.

(3) The best way to nurture the *growth of our faith* is to look beyond all *natural impossibilities*.

(4) Before we launch into the prayer of faith, the first thing that must be done is to first be in *union* with Jesus *experientially* to receive the specific *authoring* and *initiation* of faith for the object of prayer.

(5) Until we understand that our *love* for Jesus should be *unconditional*, we will never enter into the *sweet fellowship* that is kept for those who love Him without reservation.

(6) In the *pregnancy period* of faith, the object of faith is not just strengthened by needs but rather it is *energized* by God *wanting* to do something through us.

(7) Once the *seed* of faith is placed into our spirits, the desire, vision or burden for the final manifestation of the *ultimate result* of faith begins to take place.

# Chapter 3
## LEAVING THE PAST BEHIND

*Brethren, I do not count myself to have apprehended; but one thing I do, forgetting those things which are behind and reaching forward to those things which are ahead,* [14]*I press toward the goal for the prize of the upward call of God in Christ Jesus.*
**(Philippians 3:13-14)**

## In this Chapter, you will learn about:

- ➢ Forgiveness
- ➢ Past Struggles
- ➢ Faith Exploits
- ➢ Not Looking Back

## FORGIVENESS

Faith is the hand that receives the things we need from God. Everything Jesus purchased for us on Calvary can be obtained by faith. This includes salvation, healing, the fullness of the Spirit, victory over the world, the flesh, and all the powers of darkness, to mention a few. This faith only works by love.

Some people act in faith but results to nothing because they harbor bitterness against others. No progress can be attained without true forgiveness. Forgiveness is letting go of the need for revenge and releasing negative thoughts of bitterness and resentment. There are two parts to forgiveness: Repentance and Conversion.

Repentance involves a change of mind. The word "repent" means to completely change one's mind about something. When a person repents, he must first admit that he was thinking wrongly and then, he must change his whole way of thinking so that he begins to think as God thinks and also see as God sees.

Conversion involves a change of direction. To be converted means to turn around and change course. This is when a person changes his ways and acts as God instructs.

> *For if you forgive men their trespasses, your heavenly Father will also forgive you.* $^{15}$*But if you do not forgive men their trespasses, neither will your Father forgive your trespasses.*
> **Matthew 6:14-15**

The prerequisite for receiving forgiveness is to offer forgiveness to others.

Forgiveness is not easy but it is necessary for us to experience all that God has for us. It is more difficult to forgive those whom you have loved but has wronged you. Whatever the case may be, we must learn to forgive and release hurtful feelings because God freely forgives us our debt of sin in Christ.

It is important that we don't allow our past experiences of pain to color the glorious future ahead of us. We must forgive in our *heart*, *head* and *house*. It must start in our heart because out of the abundance of the heart proceeds the issues of life. Any sin residing in our heart will prevent God from hearing us when we pray to Him.

What about forgiveness in our head? People that are mentally strong have to be careful of what they let in their mind. Every effort should be made on their part to prevent negative thoughts in their head so that they can get over any unpleasant experience. People do not have to say sorry before we inwardly reconcile with them. Forgiveness is much more beneficial to the person offering it than the person receiving it.

Thirdly, we must forgive people in our household because it is difficult to forgive those who are close to us especially those living in the same house with us. Parents need to forgive their children and children need to respond in kind. Also, spouses need to forgive each other. True healing comes through forgiveness and more so, the Bible instructs us that we could be angry, but we should try to resolve it before we go to bed so as not to give place to the devil (Ephesians 4:26).

> *Husbands, love your wives, just as Christ also loved the church and gave Himself for her, $^{26}$that He might sanctify and cleanse her with the washing of water by the word, $^{27}$that He might present her to Himself a glorious church, not having spot or wrinkle or any such thing, but that she should be holy and without blemish. $^{28}$So husbands ought to love their own wives as their own bodies; he who loves his wife loves himself. $^{29}$For no one ever hated his own flesh, but nourishes and cherishes it, just as the Lord does the church.*
> **Ephesians 5:25-29**

According to the above scripture, wives should submit to their husbands as the Church reverences Christ. In essence, the church did not give up anything to receive Christ. The reason why there is an intimate relationship between the church and Christ is because He sacrificed His life for us in love.

Until a woman appreciates and embraces her husband's sacrifice by submitting to him, there wouldn't be a good connection between them. Also, disharmony between a couple or among a fellowship of believers may also be as a result of their difficultly in effectively dealing with their past struggles.

## PAST STRUGGLES

> *The sun had risen upon the earth when Lot entered Zoar. $^{24}$Then the Lord rained brimstone and fire on Sodom and Gomorrah, from the Lord out of the heavens. $^{25}$So He overthrew those cities, all the plain, all the inhabitants of the cities, and what grew on the ground. $^{26}$But his wife looked back behind him, and she became a pillar of salt.*
> **Genesis 19:23-26**

Before the destruction of Sodom and Gomorrah, God sent some angels to rescue Lot and his family, but Lot's wife was indecisive and uncertain about where she was going. She stood in the middle of the street, lingering, before she was pulled out of the forbidden place. This is why the Bible says that a double-minded man cannot receive anything from God because he is unstable in all his ways (James 1:7-8).

For us to leave something behind, we have to evaluate what is presently around us. Commitment to our past issues could prevent us from embracing what God is currently working out in our lives. So many times when we pray to God, we try to resurrect what God is killing. This is a characterization of Lot's wife, depicting a person who does not fully depend on God.

Indecisiveness to move forward comes from our familiarity with what's behind us. We might be sure of where we have been but unsure of where we are heading. Some of us are so fearful, that we will rather stay in our comfort zone than go to an unknown place. So many have over-developed senses and therefore, are always afraid of the unknown. This is uncalled for, because the Bible says:

> *For God has not given us a spirit of fear, but of power and of love and of a sound mind.*
> **2 Timothy 1:7**

In the real sense of it, we should be more afraid of what we do know than what we don't know. We know that where we are is not God's best for us. To stay in a place like that is unfruitful. Our willingness to stay in our place of ease is an indication that we don't want to receive what He has in store for us. In view of this, Apostle Paul advised us not to over focus on our past but to press forward to what lies ahead. Lot's wife was very reluctant to leave the city because she had been there for so long. All of a sudden, she remembered with nostalgia all the good times she had experienced, overlooking all the atrocities committed in the city. She looked back sentimentally. It was not that her memory failed her necessarily but she was longing for something that God did not want for her anymore. As a result, she eventually turned into a pillar of salt.

Sodom and Gomorrah was a picture of the former way of life, which are the lust of the eyes and the flesh. While unsaved, the sin we were involved in, seemed enjoyable but it made us miserable. We did not stop sinning because we wanted to, but because we knew that it was leading us to death. If we don't forsake our past sinful ways, we may not be free from the bondage of sin, which could turn us to a pillar of salt like Lot's wife.

What is a pillar of salt? The word pillar means something stationary, as a sentinel, a military outpost or a statue. A statue is a figure that has no life in it. Lot's wife became a monument of sin because she was looking back and forward at the same time. Do you wonder why people only see you where you have been? It is because you are clinging onto your past pleasures, which is preventing you from making progress, as a result becoming a statue.

The Hebrew word for salt is *meh-lakh*, which means to disappear as dust, to be tossed around and eventually becoming non-invaluable. If we don't flow with the wind of the Holy Spirit, we might become irrelevant with time.

Therefore, it is imperative to belong to a fruitful fellowship of believers so that we can complement each other and be consistent in our walk with God. No one knows it all. More so, God had ordained some people to train their fellow believers not to be complacent but to grow in the knowledge of Him so that they bring flavor to their world rather than being a pillar of salt.

> *You are the salt of the earth; but if the salt loses its flavor, how shall it be seasoned? It is then good for nothing but to be thrown out and trampled underfoot by men.*
> **Matthew 5:13**

Many people are stuck because they are not passionate in their relationship with God. It is when we get closer to God that His vision becomes clearer to us. It is then easier to develop passion for a dream that is very real to us. Hence, we let go of what was holding us down when we begin to run with this vision. As we make motion with God's idea for us, His grace is released into our lives to live victoriously.

The progress we experience as a result of our fruitful walk with Him, is not that we are smart but because the wind of grace is aiding us. The reason we are not taking steps of faith with the dream God has given us is because we find it difficult to imagine how it would work out. In order not to be stagnant, we can always start small and believe God to take us to greater heights.

We should take a cue from Lot when he pled with the angels rescuing his family from the outlawed city to escape to a nearby *little* place. He beseeched the angels because the initial place of refuge (mountain) reserved for them was too far, lest the evil overtook them. The angel granted his request and also told him to make haste, assuring him that he could not execute the judgment until they arrived at the new destination.

What God has entrusted to our care might be small initially, but when the smoke clears and the dust settles, He will take us to higher grounds. Lot was divinely insulated from destruction because his uncle, Abraham interceded for him when God revealed to him, His plan to destroy the land. This is why it is essential to fellowship with like-minded believers that stay true to God. Remember, *Iron Sharpens Iron*!

## FAITH EXPLOITS

Lot was not bothered with the material possession he had acquired in Sodom and Gomorrah because he had to leave it behind so that he could go to a small place for a period of time. This is a great lesson to learn, that we should not be perturbed by what people say about us, as long as we are following God's instruction. It may appear small at the moment, but it is enough to provide refuge for us because we are at the center of His will.

**Abraham:** It is easy to leave the things we dislike when God tells us to, but it is harder to leave what we love. In Genesis 12, God entered into a covenant with Abram and then commanded him to leave his country and his people, and go to the land He would show him.

Abraham left his familiar territory in order to *get to the promise land*. Every now and then, we might be required to leave our comfort zone into a land destined for us. Many are afraid to take a step of faith because they are unsure of what is before them.

We seemingly know that God is big enough to take us into the land He promised us, but we are not sure if we are capable of walking with Him to make that a reality. Acknowledging the greatness of God will strengthen us to press on because we can only do all things through Him.

**Jacob:** According to the book of Genesis, chapter 32, Jacob had to leave what he loved to *get a new lease on life*. When he fled from his brother, Esau, he abandoned everything he treasured, so as to be left alone to encounter God. Sometimes, it is essential to be alone, so that you can discover the real you. To be alone is different from being lonely. A person can be alone but still fulfilled.

People tend to be lonely because of a feeling of emptiness inside of them. Many single people want to be attached to others they believe will make them happy; but for them to be successful in this undertaking; they have to be comfortable in themselves. Give yourself a treat, talk to yourself if you have to, laugh at yourself if you have to, because your life will only impact others positively when you *become a better you*.

**Joseph:** This special son of Jacob fled from an alluring Egyptian woman, *to escape a lie*. He left behind his precious coat of many colors when he was tempted. He left what he cherished to save his life. Joseph's life is a good example to learn from, to show us when to run when times get unbearable.

The Bible does not tell us to stay and pray or speak in tongues when faced with evil, but it instructs us to flee from every appearance of evil (1 Thessalonians 5:22). We start to burn with the fire of passion if we stay too long in the place of temptation. This may lead us to being swallowed by sin.

If many people had run from what was enticing them, they would not be in a mess they have gotten themselves in.

**Moses:** He had to leave Egypt, where he was treated as a prince, so that God could later instruct him to *lead the Israelites out of Egypt*. He did not just leave once but actually, he left twice. The first time, he left as a fugitive because he killed an Egyptian and the second time, he left as a friend of God. Sometimes, you might have to leave a contented job that pays your bill so that you can carry out the dream God has put inside of you.

Some may need to resign so that they can lead their generation into their destinies and out of poverty to a place of abundance. The Israelites told Moses that they wished they had been left behind in Egypt because they preferred to be in the bondage of slavery (temporary ease) than to begin a new walk with God. The frustration many are confronted with presently could be that they are the ones to blaze a trail in their lineage.

**Jesus Christ:** What about our Lord Jesus Christ? He was having a good time with His Father in heaven. He did not have to be born in a manger, worry about someone criticizing Him or dying on the cross. He left His place of rest because He loved us so much and sacrificed His life for us.

> *For God so loved the world that He gave His only begotten Son, that whoever believes in Him should not perish but have everlasting life.*
> **John 3:16**

## DON'T LOOK BACK

In the process of leaving the past behind, we don't have to linger, trying to weigh other options (should we or not), because in the process of delaying, we can miss what God has planned for us. God loved Lot and his family so much that He commanded the angels to forcefully grab them to pull them out of the proscribed place.

Lot was a man who always made a decision on what was seemingly appealing. For instance, when there was a quarrel between his herdsmen and that of his uncle, Abraham, his uncle told him that there was no need for quarrel between them because they were family. Thus, he gave him options to choose from but Lot chose the option that appeared best. God renewed His covenant with Abraham when he departed from Lot. Sometimes you have to leave a Lot to enter the new life God has for you.

When Jesus came to give Himself as a sacrifice for our sins, He came to rescue us from the destructive path that we were on. Like Lot and his family, we had pitched our tents within the city limits of the wicked. That sinful choice demands judgment and possibly death. We were doomed to the same fate of Sodom and Gomorrah, but God has given us an escape route through Jesus.

He has invited us into a life that is full of hope and joy and abundance. It's a journey away from the things that are not of God. It's a journey of becoming more and more like Him as we draw closer and closer to Him. God has amazing things ahead of us that He wants to do for us, in us, and through us – right now and in the future, too.

## Leaving the Past *Behind* | 59

But Jesus reminds us in **Luke 9:62** that:

*No one, having put his hand to the plow, and looking back, is fit for the kingdom of God.*

We cannot drag our feet. We cannot turn back and secretly long for the lifestyle we once had before we came to know Him. We must put all of that behind us and move away from it. That is why Jesus Christ came to die for us, to put that past behind us. We should not allow it to be a speed bump for us as we follow Jesus up to the highest mountaintops and down through the lowest valleys.

It may not be easy but we have to make a decision to obey God. Choosing God's path may not always seem to be the best route even though it is the right one. This is so because if God be for us, who can be against us. When we leave the past, it is imperative for us not to look back. We have to be resolute enough to keep moving forward. Has the Holy Spirit urged you to "get up and move?"

At some point, we believers are called to make some changes or moves in our lives. Usually these warnings or directives come to either spare us from hardships and pain, or to place us in a better position to live out our God-ordained purpose for us and also to experience His blessings. With any move can come feelings of uncertainty, anxiety, fear, and sometimes sadness from leaving familiar people, places and routines.

Not all moves are fun and filled with joy of starting a new life. However, God loves His children and knows all, He sees when the lives we are living and the paths we are choosing are becoming destructive, hence He instructs us to change course.

As we change our ways by moving forward and accepting His will to remove us from perilous situations, we cannot help but reminisce about what we have left behind.

Sometimes we thank God for saving us and at other times we long for that place where we once felt we belonged. It is during these times that we depend solely on God by leaning on His Word to find comfort and surety in His ways. God does not want us to look back, because looking back may cost us our lives just as it did for Lot's wife.

It is not always easy to trust that God is equipped to be in full control of our lives, but it is important to recognize that sometimes trusting God is a matter of life and death. God wants us to choose life and live it abundantly. Therefore, when God tells us to move, MOVE! Obedience is better than sacrifice (1 Samuel 15:22). Even as God is bringing us out, we should not look back, but keep moving forward, because He has greatness in store for us.

Greatness is a journey that never ends, but you can start today by:

> ...*present your bodies a living sacrifice, holy, acceptable to God, which is your reasonable service. ²And do not be conformed to this world, but be transformed by the renewing of your mind, that you may prove what is that good and acceptable and perfect will of God.*
> **Romans 12:1-2**

God loves us where we are, but He doesn't want to leave us there. He wants to shape us and make us into who He has planned for us since the dawn of creation. He has amazing things He wants to accomplish through us.

However, we can only reach the potential that He has envisioned for us if we leave that past life.

Apart from forgetting the past, it is also our responsibility to surrender our vessel to Him, because it is through Him in us that we can be empowered to walk in the newness of life and be fruitful. As we daily commune with Jesus Christ through His Word and worship, past issues that we struggled with, fizzle away.

Thus, we begin to understand what God is telling us about our present and ultimately our future. It's time to turn the page to the next chapter of your life, begin the journey now!

## *Kingdom Keys*

(1) The reason why there is a relationship, where the church is *submitting* to Christ is because He *sacrificed* His life for us in love, otherwise there will be no *intimate* relationship.

(2) Commitment to our *past* issues could prevent us from embracing what God is *currently* working out in our lives.

(3) What God has entrusted to our care might be *small* initially, but when the smoke clears and the dust settles, He will take us to *higher* grounds, if we are *faithful* with the little.

(4) Jacob had to leave what he loved to *get a new lease on life*. At times, we may have to abandon everything we treasured, so as to be left alone to encounter God.

(5) Joseph *fled* from an alluring Egyptian woman, *to escape a lie*. Staying too long in the place of temptation may lead us to being swallowed by sin.

(6) God *renewed* His covenant with Abraham when he *departed* from Lot. Sometimes you have to leave a Lot to *enter* the new life God has for you.

(7) God has amazing things *ahead* of us that He wants to do for us, in us, and through us. We cannot turn *back* and secretly long for the lifestyle we once had before we came to know Him (Luke 9:62).

# Chapter 4

## BEGINNING A NEW WALK

*For we are His workmanship, created in Christ Jesus for good works, which God prepared beforehand that we **should walk** in them.*
**(Ephesians 2:10)**

## In this Chapter, you will learn about:

- ➢ Growing In Love

- ➢ Nurturing Your Devotional Life

- ➢ Receiving the Promises of God

- ➢ Building Our Father's Kingdom

## GROWING IN LOVE

In beginning a new walk with God, it is imperative to know that the most important area of our personal life and ministry is to grow in the love of God. Too many times, we concentrate on *what we are to do* but we do not realize that *why we do it* determines both the success and the eternal impact. It is possible to do ministry without the pure motivation of love for God and others. Everything that is not done out of the motivation of love is consumed in the light of eternity.

> *And though I have the gift of prophecy, and understand all mysteries and all knowledge, and though I have all faith, so that I could remove mountains, but have not love, I am nothing. ³And though I bestow all my goods to feed the poor, and though I give my body to be burned, but have not love, it profits me nothing.*
> **1 Corinthians 13:2-3**

None of us want to waste our time doing something for years and find out in eternity that all the work is considered nothing because our motivation was for self-glory. If we are ever tired of ministry, depressed or frustrated in ministry, then something is not right. We have lost our balance. The only way to restore balance back into our life and ministry is to get back into the love of God.

From the time that we were born again, a measure of Christ's love was imparted into our lives. This agape love within us needs to grow until we know the width, length, depth and height of it. It will take all of our earthly life to grow into the fullness of this love. In ministry, we need to feel the same intensity of love for people that Jesus felt when He freely gave His life on the cross for each one of us.

This intensity of love needs to grow from day to day. The highest dimension of love in the spiritual world is the pure and holy love of God. From the highest level of God's dimension, the level is lessened through the many varieties of spiritual spheres until it reaches the physical realm, which is the lowest form. Those of us who are still physically on this earth receive but a minute measure of this dimension of love.

Having been born of the Spirit of God and of love, we now need to grow into these higher dimensions. It cannot be done overnight as we need to tune a little bit more each day. As we daily yield ourselves to God, we are pitched further into a higher dimension. For this reason, it is essential that we take time daily to pray, worship and meditate on His Word, in order to allow this tuning process to take place.

We need to be honest and admit that we all don't really love people as much as God the Father and Jesus do; we are all getting there but we are not there yet. Also, when we stand to minister to people or when we pray for another person, the most important thing is to be conscious of the love of God for the people rather than to be conscious of their needs.

For what they physically need may be diverse and different, which can be purely symptoms of a greater spiritual need, but what they all really need is the love of God. Thus, we become channels of God's love, and are meeting the true need of people, not just their symptoms. As people are being restored to the God kind of love through our ministration to them, many miracles and healings and other soul and physical breakthroughs result.

The day our hearts and lives align with the same dimension of God's love, is the day that we will be doing the works and the greater works of Jesus. If our hearts and lives are not lining up with a measure of God's love in ministry and life, all that is being done would be wasted and of no eternal value. Remember, God wants us to walk and grow in love because:

> *He who does not love does not know God, for God is love.*
> **1 John 4:8**

## NURTURING YOUR DEVOTIONAL LIFE

Having established the basis of everything (Love) we do in the kingdom, I want to shed more light on how we can develop our fellowship with God. One of the first things every new believer is told to do is to have daily quality time with God. Most people understand this as finding time to pray, worship and read the Bible. The problem is that, very few books have been written about how to develop this area of our Christian life.

There are so many materials available for devotionals like a small few paragraphs of inspirational stories put together in a calendar daily format with one or two scriptures. However, in the long run, if believers depend on shallow inspirational readings for their spiritual lives, they will never really grow spiritually. It takes commitment, time and sacrifice to develop a good relationship with another person. It would take the same amount of commitment, sacrifice and time investment if we really want to develop a strong relationship with our Maker.

Christians who have made major impact on their generation began their walk with God in the daily routine of their personal devotional lives. Some spent time with God early in the morning while others preferred the night times. There is no such thing as the right time for everybody. Each one of us is unique and some of us may prefer to fellowship with God at night while others choose other times. Any time is a good time to spend time with God!

## One Hour Principle

The most important thing is to understand that we do need to devote a substantial portion of our time each day to the pursuit of God. It is highly recommended that the first few minutes of wake time or the last few minutes before sleep, be especially given to a meditation routine.

Nevertheless, how much time is the barest minimum time that we must have in order to preserve our spiritual lives? While some people would see a tithe of our day (2.4 hours a day) minimum, the Bible provides a clue as to the basic time required.

> *Then He came to the disciples and found them sleeping, and said to Peter, "What! Could you not watch with Me **one hour**?"*
> **Matthew 26:40**

During the most critical time in Jesus' ministry, when He needed His disciples to be in prayer, He called on His disciples to wait in prayer with Him for at least one hour. Unfortunately, the disciples were tired and sleepy and probably were unsuccessful in the one hour prayer request that Jesus made of them. It can be implied that the one hour requirement which Jesus requested of the disciples indicates the time we ought to spend with God in order to maintain our relationship with Him. We all know that the world is moving away from God into the lust of the flesh, the lust of the eyes and the pride of life.

When you are in a river flowing in the opposite direction from where you want to go, it takes effort to swim against the current just to maintain your position. If there is no effort to swim in the opposite direction, one would be washed out to wherever the river is flowing.

The bare minimum represents the minimum time obligation to maintain one's spirituality in a worldly environment. It is for this reason that spending at least an hour with God daily in prayer and meditation on His Word is highly advised.

## Sowing Before Reaping

We cannot expect to have a harvest if we have not taken time to sow seeds that would potentially produce the harvest. For those who live such busy lifestyles that they still see no value in giving an hour or more daily to the nurturing of their spiritual lives, we remind them that they should see this time as a valued investment that would reap benefits both spiritual and natural.

Before buying an investment portfolio that would reap great natural benefits, people take time to explore, study, research and finally invest in this. How much more should we do so in an area that would reap not just temporary benefits in this life but spiritual benefits that would last forever? The reading and application of the Word of God has benefits that would cause one to enjoy good success in this life (Joshua 1:8).

We should see devotional time as the most important investment we are making for this life and the life to come. Thus, we would have to make time for it and not just wait until free time is available.

According to the book of Deuteronomy, chapter 17, it was an obligation for kings to have a special devotional time with God. They were even required to personally create a personal copy of their own Bible and spend time reading it all the days of their lives.

Those who aspire to be leaders of nations, global corporations, and international ministries must spend quality devotional time with God and His Word if they want to achieve greatness in the kingdom of God and of men. Only God's Word provides us the instruction, correction and inspiration by which we can make our daily decisions that would affect both our lives and others around us.

An investment of time is required to help us spiritually, mentally and physically cope with all we need to accomplish each day. This time must be consistent and steady to reap a consistent and steady harvest.

## Prosperity Guaranteed

> *Blessed is the man whose delight is in the law of the Lord, And in His law he meditates day and night. ³He shall be like a tree Planted by the rivers of water, that brings forth its fruit in its season, whose leaf also shall not wither; and whatever he does shall prosper.*
> **Psalms 1:2-3**

The blessing of God comes upon the man who spends his time meditating on His Word.

The picture painted is that of a tree growing by a stream of water which one day bears fruit in its season. It is not a question of whether fruit will come but a question of when it will come, which is answered in the phrase 'in its season.'

The same promise was given to Joshua at the beginning of his leadership over the children of Israel. God promised that he will have good success if he meditated on His Word day and night. As believers in Jesus Christ, we recognize that we can do nothing without Him, and all that we are to achieve in this life, having made Him our Savior and Lord, are to be done only in Him and through Him.

Jesus frequently emphasized that we need to abide in His Word for us to bear fruit. The key to abiding in Him is to daily meditate upon His Word. The name of our Lord Jesus Christ is powerful and a refuge for the righteous but His Word is magnified above His Name (Psalms 138:2).

It is the Word that gives us faith in God's Name and is through the written Word that the spoken Word of God will be brought forth by the Holy Spirit. Heaven and earth shall pass away but the word of our Lord shall endure forever. God's promises are more sure than the expected rising of the sun every morning.

We only have to make sure that we remain good ground for His Word to be implanted into our lives daily. Dependence on the Word of God is trusting in the very source of all that is created in the Universe. By daily meditating on that Word, we are tapping into the very source of power that produced this Universe. Our success is guaranteed, if only we can hold on to His Word.

## RECEIVING THE PROMISES OF GOD

After being in devotion to God for a long while, when can we start to experience His promises? It could take a short time for some promises to manifest and longer for others. There is a group of people that lack the patience required to receive the promises, because all they want is instant gratification. They don't want what they need but they need what they want.

They want a new car, a new job and want to be highly anointed suddenly. Well, we need to surrender our will to God, in order to experience the best of Him. Before we can receive some of or all of what God has promised us, seeds have to be planted. We understand that no woman ever conceives a child today and then delivers tomorrow. We must endure a process before we receive His promise. There is a process that we all must go through in order to appreciate the next level of God's anointing.

If we are going to get our miracle or breakthrough, we must be ready to live a life of sacrifice. The Bible records of a well-to-do woman who made Prophet Elisha comfortable by building a house for him. As a result of her benevolence, God rewarded her with something she was not expecting and which her wealth could not get for her (2 Kings 4:8-17).

Like this woman, many of us were minding our own business until God decided to interrupt our agenda and impregnate us with His purpose. Our God has a way of coming in and giving us a promise that seems too big for us to handle. For instance, He told Abram that he would be the father of many nations, but he did not even have a single son at that time. God told Moses that he would lead his people out of

Egypt, but he responded that he had a speech impediment. He told Noah to build an ark because He was getting ready to send rain on earth, but before then, the world had never experienced rain.

What has He told you? God has supernatural ways of accomplishing His will through people who seemingly do not fit the description of the job. What is our role in making sure that what He told us comes to pass?

**(1) Worship Lifestyle:** One way to expedite this process of receiving His promises is to live a life of praise and worship. Praise and worship is a vehicle of intimacy with God. Praise is something we initiate but worship is something God releases. Praise is the act of us building a house for God and worship is God moving in.

Praise is one of the greatest powers of Heaven. When we praise God, we open ourselves to the healing balm of Heaven, which clears our mind, relieves stress, and refreshes our spirit. It opens a channel to the heavenlies that allows the divine blessings to pour down. Worship is a form of love. It is how we tell God how much we love Him and how thankful we are for all He does for us.

We cannot be true worshippers and excel in an intimate relationship with God just by coming to church on Sunday. It must be an everyday occurrence. When we begin to spend time with God in worship and meditation on His Word, we receive the seed of His word; then the process of conception begins in our spirit, which finally leads to the fulfillment of the promises.

**(2) Consecration:** As we grow in our relationship with God, we become very sensitive to the Holy Spirit, thus, we want to please Him so that He would not be grieved.

> *Therefore submit to God. Resist the devil and he will flee from you. ⁸Draw near to God and He will draw near to you. Cleanse your hands, you sinners; and purify your hearts, you double-minded.*
> **James 4:7-8**

Pleasing God requires that we live a consecrated life. The degree of His presence in our lives depends on our willingness to draw closer to Him. Living a consecrated life and ceasing from one's sinful habits has absolutely nothing to do with the gift of salvation, but it depends on our willingness to yield our vessel to God as a living sacrifice. We become a candidate for revival when we surrender to Him in true holiness.

Revival always requires true repentance and the forsaking of known sin. No matter how long we have been saved or in church, we all have need of repentance. How can we repent? We must acknowledge our wrongdoing and then ask God to clean us up and uphold us by His Spirit. He sustains us so that we can be on track in His plan for our lives. We have to be useful to Him in order for us to be chosen or promoted in His Kingdom. Remember, God's benchmark is diffcrent from ours.

**(3) Faithfulness:** God demands that we be faithful of His grace upon our lives. We cannot possess anything in the future until we have been proven faithful over what we have right now. What does it mean to be faithful?

A faithful person is steadfast, dedicated, dependable and worthy of trust.

The character of a faithful person does not change because of hardships. We don't really learn to be faithful until all hell has broken loose against us. When we are comfortable, it's easy to be reliable and trustworthy because nothing is disrupting our reliability. Our faithfulness is tested when we don't want to do what we must do.

God said to Abram that He would bless Him and make Him a great nation, but he had to be faithful to God despite going through a process that seemed not to be ending. This process is never designed to kill us but to refine us. The process teaches us how to appreciate the promise once it is in our possession.

Most of us reflect on the promises that God made to Abram, Moses, Joshua and the whole house of Israel but what has God promised us? Has He told us anything about our future? Has He given you an answer concerning your current dilemma? The only real reason we complain about where we are, is because we have not heard where we are heading. If we would be honest with ourselves, we will admit that we don't always have a clear picture of where we are going, but this one thing we do:

> ….*forgetting those things which are behind and reaching forward to those things which are ahead,* [14]*I press toward the goal for the prize of the upward call of God in Christ Jesus.*
> **Philippians 3:13-14**

We may not have a vivid picture of what the future holds, but we have the advantage because we know where we have been and as long as our future looks better than our past, we will keep pressing on because as believers, our path shines ever brighter unto the perfect day in glory.

The Bible says that the steps of a good man are ordered by the Lord, and also that God's Word is a lamp unto our feet and a light unto our path (Psalm 37:23, Psalm 119:105). Therefore if we get into His Word and study and apply it to our lives, then we are going to receive His promises for us.

This is because God is unbiased not to withhold any good thing from those who walk uprightly before Him. And more so, the Bible instructs us not to be discouraged in doing right, for at the appointed time, we will surely reap, if we do not give up. The choice is ours, because we have a role to play in this process.

## BUILDING OUR FATHER'S KINGDOM

In the process of waiting on God to receive the promises, what can we do, so that our lives can count for eternity? This is important because we want to be a principal participant in God's program in these last days. In the world today, there are three types of people. Firstly, there are those who want things to happen, secondly, those who watch things happen, and lastly, people who make things happen.

Most people want to be successful, but the measure of our success depends on the satisfaction with what we do. Contrary to common belief, success is not based upon how much money we make or how high our office is in the sky.

But success is measured by the ability to reach the goals set by the person trying to succeed, provided he or she is at the center of God's will.

To be successful in the Kingdom of God, there is a process to go through and a role to play. Everyone wants to be great but no one wants to do anything. To be a leader in this kingdom, we must be ready to serve, because the only way we can be what we are called to be is to firstly, do what we were called to do. Many people talk about their calling, but they never demonstrate the action of that calling.

We are not recognized just because of the title we carry, but because of the responsibility we carry out. If God calls you as an evangelist then you should be somewhere evangelizing. Or if it is the ministry of administration, you need to stay in your lane and faithfully execute your duties with commitment and excellence. Those who stay in their calling will receive their just reward.

> *For the kingdom of heaven is like a man traveling to a far country, who called his own servants and delivered his goods to them.* [20] *"So he who had received five talents came and brought five other talents, saying, 'Lord, you delivered to me five talents; look, I have gained five more talents besides them.'* [21] *His lord said to him, 'Well done, good and faithful servant; you were faithful over a few things, I will make you ruler over many things. Enter into the joy of your lord.'*
> **Matthew 25:14, 20-21**

In the above scriptures, there were three servants. One servant was given five talents, another was given two talents, and yet another was given one talent. Each was given talents according to his ability.

Just as these three servants were called by their master, so are we called by ours. The Bible says that, "for many are called, but few are chosen" (Matthew 22:14).

Many of us live our lives without knowing what we are called to be. Even if we do not know what God has called us to do, at least, we can do what we are gifted for. We should not just sit around and do nothing. God only reveals His mysteries to those who not only fear Him, but to those who are faithful stewards of His endowments in their care. We are all called *to do* and *to be*, so do not deny your calling.

The master, in the text above, gave the servants his goods so that they could trade with it for the purpose of multiplication. Likewise, God has given unto us His treasures, and our job is to be prudent with it. He gave us His talents so that we would manage it and be a blessing to our world. He wants us to work the gifts for the purpose of multiplying His Kingdom. This is the time to awake from slumber, and work the works of Him who sent us because night is coming when no man can work (John 9:4).

The first servant of the master that was given five talents, was confident and diligent in his service. He was able to take the responsibility of five talents and work them. This was a person who had the ability to multi-task and did not mind doing so. He used the resources at his disposal to make his work more productive.

The next servant who was given two talents, was also prudent in his ability to multiply his talents. He had a lot of the same characteristics as the first servant but something about this servant stood out to me. He was not intimidated by nor was he jealous of the servant who received five talents.

He worked what his master gave him and did not interfere with the dealings of his master and the other servants.

A lot of us are trying to drive our cars in someone else's lane. Why are we trying to be what God has not called us? What has God called you to do? Stop trying to be what God has called others to be. What God has for you, it is for you and no one can duplicate that. Be confident in who God called you to be and be it.

The last servant is the one who didn't multiply his talent at all, because He did not have the best interest of his master at heart. This should not be the case, because his responsibility is to receive the gifts and work them. Whatever talents God has given you, work it until it is all worked up. If God has given you a talent to build His kingdom, work that talent until you become a principal Kingdom builder.

Remember, God has a record of everything under your care and is taking note of your actions in the process of building His Kingdom. Therefore, consider your ways so that you can be counted worthy when the Master comes. I leave you with these words of our Lord Jesus Christ.

> *And behold, I am coming quickly, and My reward is with Me, to give to every one according to his work.*
> **Revelation 22:12**

## Kingdom Keys

(1) Too many times, we concentrate on *what we are to do* but we do not realize that *why we do it* determines both the success and the eternal impact.

(2) An investment of time is required to help us spiritually, mentally and physically cope with all we need to accomplish each day. This time must be consistent and steady to reap a consistent and steady harvest.

(3) The key to abiding in Him is to daily meditate upon His Word. The name of our Lord Jesus Christ is powerful and a refuge for the righteous but His Word is magnified above His Name (Psalms 138:2).

(4) By daily *meditating* on that Word, we are *tapping* into the very source of power that produced this Universe. Our success is guaranteed, if only we can hold on to His Word.

(5) We understand that no woman ever conceives a child today and then delivers tomorrow. Likewise, there is a process that we all must go through in order to appreciate the next level of God's anointing.

(6) Living a consecrated life and ceasing from one's sinful habits has absolutely nothing to do with the gift of salvation, but it depends on our willingness to yield our vessel to God daily as a living sacrifice.

(7) Many of us live our lives without knowing what we are *called to be*. Even if we do not know what God has called us to do, at least, we can do what we are *gifted for*.

# Chapter 5
## BESEECHING HIM

*Let us therefore come boldly to the throne of grace, that we may obtain mercy and find grace to help in time of need.*
**(Hebrews 4:16)**

### In this Chapter, you will learn about:

- ➢ Asking and Knocking
- ➢ Deliverance through Praise
- ➢ Seeking God Consistently
- ➢ Childlike Dependence on God

## ASKING AND KNOCKING

### Hearing God

Sometimes, we come across life's storms that only God can help us overcome. This necessitates getting the attention of God. In order to get His attention, we must be desperate because He hears those who are daring enough to do what others are too dignified to do. We must learn how to hear!

> *Now they came to Jericho. As He went out of Jericho with His disciples and a great multitude, blind Bartimaeus, the son of Timaeus, sat by the road begging. $^{47}$And when he heard that it was Jesus of Nazareth, he began to cry out and say, "Jesus, Son of David, have mercy on me!" $^{48}$Then many warned him to be quiet; but he cried out all the more, "Son of David, have mercy on me!" $^{49}$So Jesus stood still and commanded him to be called…*
> **Mark 10:46-49**

While Jesus and his disciples were leaving Jericho, Bartimaeus heard that Jesus was passing by, and he immediately cried out to Him. It is important for our spiritual ears to be sensitized, in order to hear Him clearly, especially because we cannot always see Christ physically.

Generally, when there is a deficiency in one of our senses there is usually a proficiency in another one. It is worse when people are both blind and deaf. They can't see where they are going; neither can they hear someone giving directions on where to go. The challenge of most people is that they can hear everything else but God.

They know the latest gossip, hottest hip-hop song and who is having an affair or who is not. How? Because they heard it from someone or somewhere. Most of what we hear is not true or is exaggerated. We have to be careful what we allow people to tell us because it may hinder the truth we really need to hear.

Jesus asked His disciples in Matthew 16:13, "Who do men say that I am?" They responded with, some say you are Jeremiah or one of the prophets. Then He asked them, "Who do you say that I am?" They were hesitant to respond as if they did not know. Peter who was inspired by God the Father answered and said, "You are the Christ, Son of the living God!" We must be careful not to miss who He really is based on listening to others' opinions of Him. We must hear from God for ourselves and learn to block out what others think of Him especially when it is not true!

## Looking Up To Jesus

While Bartimaeus was wailing and asking Jesus for mercy, the crowd tried to stop him. They did not care whether he found help or not. Today, the crowd still tries to shut the mouths of those who cry out to God for help. Despite the people's criticism, he merely cried out the more. He needed help, and he found the only One who could help him. He was not satisfied until he caught Jesus' attention.

We should not let the crowd stop us from crying out to God because there is no one else to turn to when we are in desperate need of help. Bartimaeus had faith that Jesus would meet his need. As soon as he found that Jesus was calling him, he cast off his garment and ran to meet Him.

Many people run helter-skelter for help, looking everywhere except God. They have their faith in the prayers of others, without praying themselves or having any faith in Jesus. However, if they would put their faith in Jesus and seek for His help, they would find the answer they needed.

> *Jesus said, "I am the way, the truth, and the life. No one comes to the Father except through Me."*
> **John 14:6**

Fix your eyes on Jesus and your needs will be met, for it is the power of God that heals and delivers. He works through others many times, but it is not that person who heals or sets us free; it is Him. His power is manifest when we exercise our faith in Him and His Word. It was Bartimaeus' faith in Jesus Christ that made him whole. He was not looking to those around him nor did he let anything discourage him.

He cried unto the Lord in faith and in the end, he received his sight. No doubt, Bartimaeus must have heard the stories of Jesus healing other blind people and how He had caused the lame to walk and the deaf to hear. These stories produced faith in his heart and caused him to cry to Jesus with all his might.

## Defying All Odds

As we truthfully reach out to God with all our strength, religious people may want to discourage us, telling us we are going against the norm. This is because they often have a difficult time understanding the ardent emotions of charismatic fervor. They have become satisfied with the status quo of their life, and are turned off by a loud noise and shout. They want everything to be conducted with dignity and respect.

So they use fear and intimidation to dampen the emotions and calm the vocal outbursts of those who are desperate for a touch from God. Nevertheless, they forget that desperate people will do desperate things. One of the most degrading sins in all of humanity is the sin of familiarity.

When people have categorized and labeled you in their own minds, they refuse to give you freedom to change your station in life. It's as though they are comfortable with your infirmities as long as you stay where they put you. They don't want you to make any noise, but a heart that is overflowing with the efficacious force of faith cannot be silenced. It can only cause one to be bold and persistent.

Sometimes, we need to make a little noise to stand out from the rest of the crowd and lift our voice in faith to God, who is the only one who can break the strongholds that have kept us bound. There will come a time, in all of our lives, when we no longer see ourselves as the defeated person asking for handouts.

We become aware of a higher destiny that resides within our heart, telling us that God has something greater in store for us. As a result of this, we cry out and reach out for a life-changing encounter with God. We must be prepared to withstand the negative rebuke from people who have no faith.

Possessing an unrelenting faith in the life changing power of God is one of the central truths of receiving from God. In God's kingdom, nothing is gained by passively sitting still and consenting to the problems of life. He wants us to ask and keep asking until He responds to us.

This is the reason Jesus instructs us to knock and keep on knocking until the door opens. To knock once and then retire in defeat is a clear indication that what we desire is not yet entrenched in a heart of faith.

## DELIVERANCE THROUGH PRAISE

You might have prayed and prayed and nothing seems to be working. Then, it is time to change your negative perspective into a positive one. Lift your hands toward heaven and start singing praises to God. You may be feeling you have nothing to praise God for because you are so miserable. That may appear to be true, but why not try praising God for just who He is.

God is still God no matter what we are going through because He is the same yesterday, today, and forever (Hebrews 3:18). Praising God in the worst of times proves that we know who He is, and what He can do. We must not allow our perspective of God to change just because we find ourselves in adverse situations. Our God is the Most High no matter what we are going through.

We can take a cue from Paul and Silas.

> *And when they had laid many stripes on them, they threw them into prison, commanding the jailer to....$^{24}$....put them into the inner prison and fastened their feet in the stocks. $^{25}$But at midnight Paul and Silas were praying and singing hymns to God, and the prisoners were listening to them. $^{26}$Suddenly there was a great earthquake, so that the foundations of the prison were shaken; and immediately all the doors were opened and everyone's chains were loosed.*
> **Acts 16:23-26**

Paul and Silas were beaten, thrown in a prison and chained up. If anyone had a reason to say there is no way out, they sure did. Nevertheless, they approached their unpleasant situation, firstly by praying. After they told God their problem, they handed it over to Him and began to sing. In the midst of all their havoc, they sang! They could have given up because there seemed to be no way out of their situation. Instead they decided to praise God because they knew who their God was.

They did not allow their condition to change their perspective of Him. In the end, the just God heard them and set them free. He hears ours prayers and also delights in our praises. Prayer followed with praise is powerful and proves that we know who He is. It shows our faith in Him. If Paul and Silas had simply said there is no way out, they would have stayed in bondage.

A negative response to the contrary situation we sometimes find ourselves in may cause us to stay in the dilemma or can also give place to the devil. We cannot be praying to God to deliver us out of a mess and then keep talking about how awful everything is. Paul and Silas prayed and allowed their actions to glorify God. They reacted positively to their situation, and as a result they were liberated.

We can train ourselves to react positively to our situations as well. For example, when a problem arises, many of us find ourselves saying, "This is a bad situation, there is no way out." By saying that, we are implying that God cannot turn the situation around. As children of God, we need to know who our God is and what He can do for us. With God, all things are possible and every contrary situation will work for our good if our life is pleasing to Him.

Therefore, it is imperative that we train our thoughts to line up with the Word of God. His Word helps us keep the positive attitude we need to handle any bad situations that may arise. If we can think negatively, then we can also think positively. Positive thinking is knowing that no matter what, God will deliver us. The transformation of our thought pattern is not something that can be achieved in a day, but we can start the journey today, by meditating on God's Word and allow it to saturate our entire being.

The devil is all out to hamper God's program for as many as he can deceive but our responsibility is to surrender our lives to God. The degree of deliverance we can experience depends on our level of yieldedness to God and His Word. When we become an embodiment of God, the devil and his agents do not have any option but to flee from us.

When we praise God we create a space for Him to live and to be comfortable in. The Bible tells us that God inhabits the praises of His people. We know that the devil cannot exist or prevail where God lives. As we become consistent *praisers*, we will find deliverance through our praise!

## SEEKING GOD CONSISTENTLY

We all want God's attention! There is no believer that does not have the desire for God to take notice of him or her. This is especially true when we want or need something from Him. It might be the miracle of salvation of a loved one or the miracle of a financial blessing or an emotional healing. Whatever the case may be, how do we get the attention of God? We can get hold of Him by consistently seeking after Him.

For instance, the Book of Acts, chapter 10 tells us of a man who lived in Caesarea, an Italian centurion, who was devout and loved God. This man caught God's attention to the point that He sent His angel to him because his prayers had come up as a memorial offering before Him. This man's prayer touched God so much that He changed the custom.

Until that time God had reserved His relationship solely for those who were from Israel, but not for the gentiles. In fact, on one occasion Jesus himself likened a gentile to a dog (Matthew 15:21-28). In the process of bringing salvation to the gentiles, God also revealed a vision to Peter so that he could minister to them. He had to change his way of thinking because he believed otherwise.

Salvation came to the house of Cornelius because God visited him. What had aroused God's awareness of him to the point that He would cross ethnic boundaries? What was it that caused God to revolutionize societal guidelines and reach out to a gentile?

There are **three** things that are mentioned in the **character** description of Cornelius that gives us a clue why God encountered him.

The Bible says in **Acts 10:1-4**,

> *There was a certain man in Caesarea called Cornelius….²a **devout** man and one who feared God with all his household, who gave alms **generously** to the people, and **prayed** to God always. ³About the ninth hour of the day he saw clearly in a vision an angel of God coming in and saying to him, "Cornelius!"⁴….Your prayers and your alms have come up for a memorial before God.*

**(1) Devotion:** He was a Godly man who held God in awe. His entire house also respected God, holding Him in high admiration and wonderment. As a result, God visited them, by sending his angel to let him know that his prayers and generosity had touched heaven.

He was able to get hold of God because he prayed consistently. In view of this, Jesus tells us in Luke 18 that, "...men ought always to pray, and not to faint." Fainting does not mean to pass out. It means to lose heart or lack courage. In this same passage, Jesus tells the story of a woman who went to the unjust judge. Although he refused to help her initially, she continued to see him until he met her need.

Jesus then said that, God would meet the needs of his people if they would continue in faith to ask of Him. Cornelius prayed continuously until God answered. How many times do we stop praying just before we hear from God? How many times do we lose heart and give up just before the angel knocks on our door?

**(2) Generous Giving:** The angel of the Lord also mentioned to Cornelius that his generous giving also caught the responsiveness of God. God offers to us the benefit of giving in addition to us praying to Him. In fact, in the book of Malachi, God said if we do not give as instructed, He would curse us. If we do give, He will open the windows of heaven and pour out blessings that will overflow our ability to contain them. This blessing is not just financial but the kind that covers every aspect of our lives.

**(3) Consistency:** The third point the angel mentioned was that Cornelius had been faithful. He had prayed and given continuously. It was not a onetime occasion. His prayers and giving were not just a passing fad or an emotional high. It was his way of life. This is why the Bible advises us in **Hebrews 10:35-36**.

> *Therefore do not cast away your confidence, which has great reward. $^{36}$For you have need of endurance, so that after you have done the will of God, you may receive the promise.*

Paul, the apostle was telling us to be faithful. We need to keep that bold assurance which we have in God. He encourages us to cheerfully, with hopeful endurance be consistent so that we can receive the promise.

The angel told Cornelius that his giving, his praying and his consistency had become a memorial before God. It kept alive the memory of his needs. The beauty of the story is that when Cornelius caught the attention of God, not only his household but every gentile from that point on was given the opportunity for salvation.

If we continue on faithfully; if we refuse to lose heart, we will get God's attention. If we maintain our confidence and trust in God, we will encounter Him. There is no doubt that He loves and cares for us dearly, but He is a just God who only rewards people that diligently seek Him.

## CHILDLIKE DEPENDENCE ON GOD

Almost everyone who believes in God prays and every Christian who has needs prays. Yet, each prayer has a different impact and some do not even go beyond the earthly sphere because they are too carnal. Therefore, it is crucial that we know the **essentials** of prayer because it involves more than making our needs known to God, for God knows all that we need before we pray.

**(1) Eternal Impact:** Every prayer, every cry, every desire that constitutes both verbal and silent prayer is heard by God and is evaluated based on its eternal value. Thus, all prayers go through purification and evaluation process, with those purest having the greatest eternal impact. This does not mean that it is the most visibly spiritual people whose prayers have such eternal impact. However, it also includes prayers of innocent children and pure hearted unknown Christians.

Included in this purification process is the motivation for the prayers. For this reason, some prayers seem to take time because its drive and understanding of the eternal impact is impure. Through time with the help of the Holy Spirit, God firstly works within the one who utters the prayer until the prayer uttered becomes purified.

Besides that, some prayers have a time schedule of answer. This does not mean that the prayer is answered based on the merit of the person but rather that the person who prays has not appropriated the same purity of Christ into his or her life. In order to appropriate the finished work of Christ as our basis, it has to be Christ praying through us.

Christ loves us so much that He sent the Holy Spirit to help us pray the right way.

> *Likewise the Spirit also helps in our weaknesses. For we do not know what we should pray for as we ought, but the Spirit Himself makes intercession for us with groanings which cannot be uttered.* [27]*Now He who searches the hearts knows what the mind of the Spirit is, because He makes intercession for the saints according to the will of God.*
> **Romans 8:26-27**

If Christ indeed is praying through us by His Spirit, how many of our prayers would be the same in terms of its content and motivation? The fact that prayer is answered based on its eternal impact and not merely for its temporal effect, does not mean that God is not interested in our daily needs or earthly concerns but rather our needs are met as a plus to the eternal impact answers that we receive.

**(2) Faith in God's Love:** The scriptural ground for all prayers is the love of God. This assurance of the Father's love is the basis for all our ability to have faith in His Word. Hence, before one utters any prayers, one should become conscious of the greatness of God's love for us. It is this confidence of God's love for us that renders us more than conquerors. It is also out of this confidence that we, in turn, are able to love God and our neighbor.

Thus, having the ability to pray with the confidence that all things work out for good to those who love God boosts our faith in the place of prayer. Consequently, all answered prayers are purely the expression of God's love for us. For some people, they want their prayers to be answered before they have confidence in God's love for them. This renders their prayers powerless. We need to *first* have confidence in God's love *before* we pray. How do we have this confidence?

By looking at the finished work of Christ. Christ's finished work speaks one phrase aloud 'God loves us.' For our prayers to be effective, we *must* be *fully assured* of God's love for us through Christ. After being assured of this love, it stirs our love towards Him.

Think of it this way, if God did nothing else for us, but gave His son for us; if He did not answer one more prayer (which, of course, He won't), if nothing else is brought forth for us, all that He did on the cross would have been enough. We should be willing to crawl on our knees across an ocean of broken glass or scale a Mount Everest of thorns, in declaration of our love in response to His love, for all that Jesus did for us on the cross.

Ironically, it is when we are so *filled* with God's love, and so *immersed* in love towards Him and our neighbor that we desire *nothing* else but to *love God* and *give* our lives for Him as a living poetry of love, that our prayers are the *most* powerful.

Thus, it is imperative that we pray:

> *That Christ may dwell in your hearts through faith; that you, being rooted and grounded in love, [18]may be able to comprehend with all the saints what is the width and length and depth and height - [19]to know the love of Christ which passes knowledge; that you may be filled with all the fullness of God. [20]Now to Him who is able to do exceedingly abundantly above all that we ask or think, according to the power that works in us, [21]to Him be glory in the church by Christ Jesus to all generations, forever and ever. Amen.*
> **Ephesians 3:17-21**

The love of God through Christ is the source of all true pure prayers and the answers given to all prayers are to further establish the love of God for us through Christ. In an ever-widening cycle, love keeps being experienced increasingly for all eternity, in this life and in the next.

**(3) Christ Consciousness:** No matter how old we are in earth years, or how experienced we are in the things of God, we are all little children to our Heavenly Father. Let us in prayer learn the true secrets of childlikeness, of total dependence on the pure love of our Father in Heaven, of pure child-like response to God's love through us for others.

We might no longer speak like a child, understand as a child or think like a child but we ought to always *trust* as a child. The secret things still belong to those with childlike trust and love towards our Father God. Of all the thoughts we think daily, of all the consciousness that we need to have every day, the *most* important consciousness and thought is that God loves us very much. This consciousness was so real and always in Paul's daily life that he declared in **Galatians 2:20**.

> *I have been crucified with Christ; it is no longer I who live, but Christ lives in me; and the life which I now live in the flesh I live by faith in the Son of God, who loved me and gave Himself for me.*

The love of God had been poured into our hearts when we gave our lives to Christ. We can grow in this pure love and Christ consciousness by regularly praying in the Spirit and also meditating on God's Word, especially on those scriptures that affirm our position in Christ. Some of those scriptures are on Pages 121-125 of this book.

## Kingdom Keys

(1) In order to *get* God's attention, we must be *desperate* because He hears those who are daring enough to do what others are too dignified to do.

(2) Sometimes, we need to make a little noise to stand out from the rest of the crowd and lift our voice in faith to God, who is the only one that can break the strongholds that have kept us bound.

(3) We must not allow our perspective of God to change just because we find ourselves in adverse situations. Our God is the Most High in spite of what we are going through.

(4) The devil is all out to hamper God's program for as many as he can deceive but our responsibility is to *surrender* our lives to God. The degree of *deliverance* we can experience depends on our level of *yieldedness* to God and His Word.

(5) If we *maintain* our *confidence* and *trust* in God no matter what, we will encounter Him. There is no doubt that He loves and cares for us dearly, but He is a just God who only rewards people that *diligently* seek Him.

(6) Regardless of how old we are in earth years, or how experienced we are in the things of God, we are all little children to our Heavenly Father. Let us in prayer learn the true secrets of *childlikeness* and total *dependence* on our Heavenly Father.

(7) It is when we are so *filled* with God's love, and so *immersed* in love towards God and our neighbor that we desire *nothing* else but to *love* Him and *give* our lives for Him as a living poetry of love, that our prayers are the *most* powerful.

# Chapter 6
## BEHAVING LIKE CHRIST

*I have been crucified with Christ; it is no longer I who live, but Christ lives in me; and the life which I now live in the flesh I live by faith in the Son of God, who loved me and gave Himself for me.*
**(Galatians 2:20)**

### In this Chapter, you will learn about:

- ➢ Waiting On the Lord

- ➢ What a Christian Life as all about

- ➢ Striving For Perfection

- ➢ Refusing to Quit

## WAITING ON THE LORD

We live in an era where it is hard for us to wait for anything. We have been overtaken by the fast food competitors and microwaveable meals. This does not stop with food but also the internet plays a major role in encouraging the lack of patience that this present generation has been lured into. We have almost everything at the click of a button. Why go to the airport and stand in a long line to purchase an airline ticket when I can purchase it online. Why go to the box office to get Los Angeles Lakers basketball tickets when I can get them in the confines of my own home.

Everyone is advertising that they have faster service than their competitor. Just because something is faster does not mean that it is better. The Bible declares that the race is not given to the swift nor the battle to the strong but to the one who endures until the end. Sometimes we need to wait for the crock pot meal. We must understand that the longer a food is prepared the more seasoned it is. The reason we have so many unseasoned Christians is because we do not like to wait through our preparation.

We have become so accustomed to the convenience created by man that we cannot wait through the process created by God. It is amazing that some people can sit for four hours to get their hair done but cannot wait for one hour to hear from God. Everyone enjoys convenience but we have neglected to realize that convenience has fed our hunger to get everything quick and in a hurry.

Since we are so used to getting things when we want them without waiting, we now have trouble with God when we have to wait for our healing, deliverance or our financial breakthrough.

Could this be the reason so many Christians give up on God when they don't get their way? Could it be that our society has birthed some spoiled, ungrateful, milk drinking Christians that cannot handle a season of waiting?

Our desire today should be, Lord teach us how to wait. Waiting means to remain in readiness or expectation. In other words, no matter how dire our situation is, we should endure in anticipation that our God is on the way to liberate us. Sometimes, when we present our concerns to Him again and again, we might grow tired of waiting. It soon begins to feel like our prayers are falling on deaf ears.

It is in these periods of waiting on His Word that we begin to activate His divine nature in us so that we can start behaving like Christ. More so, the Bible instructs us that:

> ...*those who wait on the Lord Shall renew their strength; they shall mount up with wings like eagles, they shall run and not be weary, they shall walk and not faint.*
> **Isaiah 40:31**

Many people in the Body of Christ are losing their battles because they are not waiting on God enough for their strength to be invigorated; thus their ideas and creativity become stale. The carnal reaction is to always want to take control and just do the best we can but as we wait on Him, we should ask the Spirit to fill us, empowering and directing us aright.

This does not mean our circumstances will change instantly, but we begin to develop the character of Christ. The experience of waiting on God reminds us that our reality as Christians is not within our apparent circumstances, but rather in the truth of Christ's love and life in us. This gives us hope as **Romans 8:28** assures us that:

> *…all things work together for good to those who love God, to those who are the called according to His purpose.*

It is not in our abilities to know the time or way in which God will work things out. Our role here is to trust Him and wait with hope as He brings about to completion the good work He began in each of our lives. God gives us the freewill to either wait on Him or not, but it is our choice to act in willful obedience.

Adam and Eve were given complete free will. They were given many provisions in the garden so that they would not need to partake in the forbidden fruit. However, they chose to not exercise restraint and instead disobeyed God's command. When we choose to wait on His will and timing, we renounce Adam's fallen actions and step out in obedience towards God.

There is purpose in the process. Waiting on God forces us to look to Him. It casts our eyes rightly to Christ as the source of our faith and the assurance of our salvation. It reminds us that Christ's death and life is the reason we can be filled with and empowered by the Holy Spirit.

Trials cause us to persevere by deepening our knowledge of God and relying on Him more intentionally. Thus, we become more mature and established in Him. Standing patiently when we wait on Him does not mean that we should be stuck at a standstill. But that we keep putting on the full armor of God, so that we can extinguish all the fiery darts of the enemy.

Holding our ground by being obedient to God while waiting is not passive, because God richly rewards us when we patiently claim ground for His Kingdom. In the process of waiting, we can rest on Him to give us the strength to bear our circumstances and also use the time to grow in intimacy with Him.

## WHAT A CHRISTIAN LIFE IS ALL ABOUT

### Abiding in the Vine

The story was told of a believer who was a tremendous testimony to all the people who knew him. He had a daily Bible-reading booklet; and if he did not get a chance to witness to someone about Jesus Christ each day, he would write, "No fruit" in the margin of that particular day. This gave the impression that it is exclusively when we tell others about Christ that we only bear fruit.

However, in addition to spreading the gospel of the kingdom, it is imperative that we develop the character of Jesus, so that our witnessing can be more effective. This necessitates that we abide in Him because the Christian life is all about being in union with Christ so that we can bear fruit unto holiness. It gladdens the heart of the Father when we produce fruit of His kind.

> *Abide in Me, and I in you. As the branch cannot bear fruit of itself, unless it abides in the vine, neither can you, unless you abide in Me. ⁵ "I am the vine, you are the branches. He who abides in Me, and I in him, bears much fruit; for without Me you can do nothing.*
> **John 15:4-5**

He does not want to just have vine branches but abundantly fruitful branches, that give fruit to their full potential. The realization is that we are only a vessel, meant to contain and reflect Jesus Christ. He produces the fruit, not us. Fruit bearing is a manifestation of the Christ in us. We are just the vessels that are being used by God. To be the container of Jesus Christ is to allow Him to do the producing.

Bearing fruit is not what we do but who we become in Him. As we commune with Christ through prayer and the meditation on His Word, the fruit bearing process takes place effortlessly. For instance, an apple tree that appears to be dead in January is covered with fragrant blossoms within a couple of months. In the fall, it is full of delicious apples. It stands there tall, beautiful, spontaneously producing what it was made to produce by its Creator.

Bringing forth fruit presupposes that we are abiding in the Vine (Christ). It is impossible for a branch to bring forth fruit, unless it abides in the vine. So likewise, it is our union with Christ that can make us (the branches) to bring forth good fruit. Ministering and pursuing the good works that God prepared for us demands therefore a passionate relationship with our Lord Jesus Christ.

## The Pruning

The focus is not so much on the works but on Christ, and through our union with Him, the fruit comes forth. As we bear fruit, He will prune us so that we can bear much more fruit. What is pruning? Pruning is the practice of removing non-productive or unwanted portions from a plant. The purpose of pruning is to shape the plant by directing its growth, to maintain its health and also increase the yield or quality of flowers and fruit it produces.

Proper pruning is as much a skill as it is an art, since badly pruned plants can become diseased or grow in undesirable ways. Every plant needs a farmer that will prune it and direct its growth to the desirable way and nurture it so that it brings more fruit. The same is true for us as branches of the Vine because we cannot grow without it. We have Father God as the farmer, who takes care of the pruning.

He watches as a good and careful farmer. He intervenes, by guiding our development, removing obstacles and purging us so that we can be more fruitful. Is this not wonderful? It is our responsibility to abide in the Vine and it is the Father's job to take care of any pruning that is necessary to increase our fruitfulness. What can we do to effectively cooperate with God since we know that He will surely do His part?

## Fruit Bearing Process

Let's take a cue from the Word of our Master, Jesus Christ in **Mark 4:26-29**.

> *And He said, "The kingdom of God is as if a man should scatter seed on the ground, <sup>27</sup>and should sleep by night and rise by day, and the seed should sprout and grow, he himself does not know how. <sup>28</sup>For the earth yields crops by itself: first the blade, then the head, after that the full grain in the head. <sup>29</sup>But when the grain ripens, immediately he puts in the sickle, because the harvest has come."*

Jesus used an example of seed, time, and harvest, to illustrate truths about how His Word works in us to bear fruit. First, He taught that God's Word has to be planted like a seed in our hearts. Just as a seed does not release its life until it is planted into the ground, His Word will not liberate us until it is planted in our hearts. Having the Bible on our tables, in our hands, or in our heads is not sufficient; we have to meditate on it so that it can be planted in our hearts.

Second, the man in Jesus' parable, who sowed the seed, took his time to observe the process of growth. It takes time for a seed to germinate. We cannot plant a seed one day and expect to see it growing the next day. Just because there is nothing visible above ground does not mean the seed is not growing. We must have faith that the seed will do what it was designed by God to do, producing its fruit in its time.

God's Word works the same way. When we meditate on it for one day, we cannot expect to see results the next day. We cannot meditate on His Word one day and then live differently the other six days. That's like digging up the seed from the ground. We have to continually soak ourselves in His Word so as to be energized by its nutrients.

> *If you abide in Me, and My words abide in you, you will ask what you desire, and it shall be done for you. [8]By this My Father is glorified, that you bear much fruit; so you will be My disciples.*
> **John 15:7-8**

The Word is a seed that contains the very life of God. When it is planted and left in our heart, it will release that life. The only effort on our part is to take the time to plant the seed. Then, the Christlikeness we are trying to attain comes without struggle as the seed of His Word takes root in our heart. This is such a simple truth that most people have missed it.

Many are looking for some spectacular divine encounter that will transform their lives instantly. They want to microwave their miracle rather than allow the time for the seed to produce fruit. In the natural, we know that we cannot have a harvest without planting seeds, but in the spiritual, Christians try it all the time. Instead of going to the Word and meditating on it themselves, they run to someone who has spent time in the Word and ask them for help.

It is an attempt to shortcut the process of seed, time, and harvest. Then, if they don't see the desired results, they get confused and offended. God can meet needs through the faith of others, but it is temporary and His secondary way of touching us. He wants us to take the seed of His Word and plant it in our hearts where it will naturally and effortlessly produce the changes we long for.

Have you ever seen an apple tree groan and travail to produce apples? Certainly not! It is the nature of an apple tree to bring forth its fruit. It is our nature to produce fruit spiritually, just as it happens naturally. We do have a part to play however. God has never planted a seed or tended the field for anyone. That is the natural part that we must do. It is up to us to consistently plant His Word in our hearts, abide in it, and then water and nourish it with prayer.

If we make that effort, God will use the life in the seed of His Word to do the rest. Our lives will naturally change. The Christian life is truly not hard; it is actually easy if we are abiding in God's Word. The Word will transform us so that God's perfect will for us comes to pass. That's the promise of His Word in Romans 12:2. Being spiritually minded is being Word minded. The seed is God's Word.

The soil is our hearts and the fruit that we all long for is the godly transformation into the image of Christ.

## STRIVING FOR PERFECTION

I remember in year 2008, men and women alike all across America were glued to their television to watch the highly anticipated Super Bowl XLII football game between the New York Giants and the New England Patriots. The Patriots were already billed as one of the greatest teams in NFL history. The Patriots were not only competing for a fourth Super Bowl title, but they were aiming to become the first team in NFL history to achieve a 19-0 record.

Before the game started, the special day could either turn out to be the greatest day or the greatest upset in sports history. The Patriots were in pursuit of perfection. As I watched ESPN all week being an avid sports fan, I began to get revelation from the scripture, comparing David, the son of Jesse with Tom Brady of New England Patriots, the 2007 NFL Most Valuable Player (MVP).

They both had to overcome being overlooked. Tom Brady was the last quarterback picked in the 2000 NFL Draft. David was the last son to come into the house to be anointed by Prophet Samuel. David was overlooked seven times before he was called on and Tom Brady was overlooked 198 times before he heard his name called. David and Tom Brady at the time they started their journeys were the least likely to be in a position to pursue perfection.

I am sure that the owners of the Patriots could not imagine that a last round pick would become the MVP of the league.

He not only became the MVP of the league but he also set the record for the most touchdown passes ever in one season. As you are reading this book, even though you might have been overlooked before, you are still very valuable because God created you uniquely and perfectly with a special plan and purpose.

If we are going to pursue that perfection, there are some things that we must consider. It is not how we start but how we finish that really matters. Although we might fall sometimes in the process, it still does not stop us from getting up and continuing the pursuit of perfection. As a matter of fact, our mistakes teach us and fuel us to do better after we have learned from them.

Tom Brady was able to become MVP in the NFL because he was not discouraged after being passed over several times but kept practicing and playing by the rules of the game. In our Christian vocation, God has set guidelines in His Word for us to follow, as we strive for perfection in our walk with Him. His Spirit is also available in us but we have to continually yield to it so as to keep it activated. How do we go about achieving perfection in God's perspective?

> *Therefore you shall be perfect, just as your Father in heaven is perfect.*
> **Matthew 5:48**

How do we attain the perfection Jesus is talking about? When perfection is mentioned, people immediately become uncomfortable. None of us are flawless. We all make mistakes, we all do and say things we are sorry for. So what is the perfection our God is referring to in the above verse?

The other words we can use for perfect in this context are: complete, of full age. How do we come to completion? How do we arrive at full age, or maturity?

We grow up in Christ by dying to the flesh and carnal thinking, and learning to live totally under the guidance of the Holy Spirit. That is why Christ gave His life for us. He paid the price for mankind to have the opportunity to become fully reconciled to the Father. When we think of perfection as an unattainable goal, we are rejecting the truth of what Jesus' sacrifice bought and paid for.

We know how to be accepted and fit in with those around us. What we have to learn is how to allow the Holy Spirit to change us into the new creature in Christ we are called to become. This is accomplished by the renewing of our mind. It takes a major mind renovation to change the way we think. To be fully transformed means that we have fully died to our flesh, and now live by the power of the Spirit.

Today, there seems to be an almost casual acceptance of all of our shortcomings. We will never become Christ-like if that is the way we think. The faith many exhibit is one of defeated acceptance, rather than a desire to walk in the fullness. We are either growing up in Christ, or we are deteriorating. The truth is that there is no middle ground in following Christ. There is no comfortable fence we can sit ourselves upon to watch and see how things will work out.

How do we accomplish this? We have to believe, we have to obey, and we have to grow in the reverential fear of God. How ironic is it that we fear everything but God? We fear the devil, and give him credit for every unpleasant thing in our lives.

What we fail to comprehend is that he was already defeated. If we would grow up in Christ, if we would live by the power of the Spirit instead of the power of our flesh, we would walk in victory and resisting him would no longer be an insurmountable obstacle. Jesus overcame, and by the power of Christ in us, we too, can overcome.

We fear what others think. We are more concerned about the approval and admiration of others, than we are concerned with pleasing God. Obedience to what instructs us will not endear us to others. The heart of man without God has not changed down through the centuries. People today are just as adept at rejecting the True Word of the Lord as they ever were.

We might fall several times, but we have to keep coming to God to strengthen us for the journey. The true perfection is when we evaluate our lives regularly with His Word and also make necessary adjustments in areas where we stumble. As we do that by His Spirit, we are maturing in Christ, moving from infants, where we feed on milk, to eating the solid food of His Word.

We are more than conquerors through Christ in us and as we seek for perfection by the power of the Holy Spirit, we have to consistently:

> *Examine yourselves as to whether you are in the faith. Test yourselves. Do you not know yourselves, that Jesus Christ is in you?—unless indeed you are disqualified.*
> **2 Corinthians 13:5**

## REFUSING TO QUIT

In our Christian journey, we have to admit that at times we do not want to continue. There have been some days where we feel like quitting. The pressures of life are weighing down some people because the vision they received from God for a specific assignment is not forthcoming. On the road to Gethsemane, Jesus refused to cave in to discouragement so as to get to the cross, so likewise we should not give up but keep pressing toward the goal which God set before us.

Some are even upset, not with themselves or family or friends, but with God. This should not be the case because it is only God we can depend on to bring our dreams to fruition. It is not strange to feel that way, because even one of the greatest Old Testament prophets called Jeremiah experienced such emotional turmoil to the extent that he wanted to quit.

This was a man whom God ordained a prophet from his mother's womb and was told by God not to say that he was a child, because He has put His Words in his mouth. Many of us can empathize with Jeremiah because we have been there. We know that God has called and anointed us into what we are doing, yet it seems as if heaven is closed and as a result, we are in a place of loneliness and depression.

Jeremiah heard from God and prophesied to the people exactly what God told him. It appeared that God was not backing him up because the people did not respond accordingly. He forgot to realize that God works in ways we cannot always fathom. Jeremiah allowed his frustration and anxiety to get him so down in the dumps that he said:

> *I will not make mention of Him, nor speak anymore in His name. But His word was in my heart like a burning fire shut up in my bones; I was weary of holding it back, And I could not.*
> **Jeremiah 20:9**

Many of us have been in situations when we know it is right to fast and pray but we do not feel like doing it. We know we should be studying His Word but are weighed down with life's issues. It is not that we do not know the right thing to say or do, but we are discouraged because our expectations are not being met. Thus, we are resolving to quit.

I am not at all referring to backsliding. Backsliding and quitting are completely different. It does not talk about going back to the old corrupt ways which we were delivered from. But it refers to getting so tired of doing what we know God has called us to do and because we are not seeing the right results, we want to throw in the towel.

One of the greatest frustrations of Christians is that, when we receive a promise from God, we expect it to come to pass in a short while. This is not always the case. Many times, pressure comes before we receive any of God's promises. Wanting to quit is not all bad because if we ever desire to quit doing anything, it must mean that we are involved in a worthwhile venture.

No one who is sitting idle ever has the urge to quit because he or she is not involved in anything. Great men and women of God have all felt like quitting. Abraham who was called the friend of God, at a time wanted to quit. David, a man after God's own heart wanted to quit when he said:

> *Oh, that I had wings like a dove! I would fly away and be at rest. $^7$Indeed, I would wander far off, and remain in the wilderness. Selah $^8$I would hasten my escape from the windy storm and tempest.*
> **Psalm 55:6-8**

Elijah wanted to quit when Jezebel was on his trail. Jonah wanted to quit when God told him to go to Nineveh. Moses, a man who spoke with God face to face wanted to quit many times but he did not. What is significant in all these cases is that none of these men quit doing what God called them to do. What can we do so that our story will not be different?

We can learn from Paul, the Apostle, who wrote two-thirds of the New Testament, despite being stoned, dragged out of the city by a horse or mule, and left as dead. He was not dejected; instead he focused on his assignment.

He wrote:

> *Brethren, I do not count myself to have apprehended; but one thing I do, forgetting those things which are behind and reaching forward to those things which are ahead, $^{14}$I press toward the goal for the prize of the upward call of God in Christ Jesus.*
> **Philippians 3:13-14**

It is imperative that we leave the past behind and also cast away every weight that slows us down in our journey to destiny. Discouragement might set in sometimes but it is in our own interest to keep **looking up to Jesus** (our Perfect Model), who will always strengthen us to finish the race with flying colors.

> **Looking unto Jesus**, *the author and finisher of our faith, who for the joy that was set before Him endured the cross, despising the shame, and has sat down at the right hand of the throne of God.*
> **Hebrews 12:1-2**

## *Kingdom Keys*

(1) Many have become so *accustomed* to the convenience created by *man* that they *cannot wait* through the process created by *God*. It is in these periods of waiting on Him that we begin to *activate* His *divine nature* in us so that we can start *behaving* like Christ.

(2) Having the Bible on our tables, in our hands, or in our heads is not sufficient; we have to *meditate* on it so that it can be *planted* in our hearts.

(3) The Word is a *seed* that contains the *very life* of God. When it is *planted* and left in our heart, it will *release* that life. The only effort on our part is to take the time to plant the seed.

(4) Although we might *fall* sometimes in the process, it still does *not stop* us from getting up and continuing the *pursuit of perfection*. As a matter of fact, our mistakes teach us and fuel us to do better after we have learned from them.

(5) When we *evaluate* our lives regularly with God's *Word* and also make the necessary *adjustments* in areas where we stumble, we are *maturing* in Christ, moving from infants, where we feed on milk, to eating the solid food of His Word.

(6) It is imperative that we *leave the past behind* and also cast away every weight that slows us down in our journey to destiny. Discouragement might set in sometimes but it is in our own interest to keep *looking up to Jesus* (our Perfect Model).

(7) On the road to Gethsemane, Jesus *refused* to cave in to discouragement so as to get to the cross, so likewise we should *not give up* but keep *pressing* toward the goal which God set before us.

# *Epilogue*

God's desire for all who know Him is for them to become more like Christ. We do this by first growing in our knowledge of Christ. It stands to reason that we cannot grow to be like someone we do not know. The deeper our knowledge of Christ, the deeper our understanding of Him, and the more like Him we become.

Going through *Just BE!* you must have found out that becoming a man who walks with God takes a process. This transformational process requires both His divine power and our collaboration. Therefore, it is beneficial for us to cooperate with the Holy Spirit. This course occurs over an entire lifetime in Christ. Only when we have entered Heaven for eternity with God does this process reach its culmination.

This book revealed that this process starts with us discovering our root in Christ and also surrendering to Him so that we can take on His nature. This involves fellowshipping with others of like precious faith so as to complement each other. Doing this will help us to leave the past behind and focus on the main thing, the Word of God, which will strengthen our faith in Him.

A new fruitful walk with God demands that we nurture our devotional life so that we can mature to receive the promises of God for us. This leads us to deepening our relationship with Him by solely depending on Him like a child. It does not stop there, but it also involves us striving for perfection in Christ and also stretching forward to complete the race set before us.

*Just BE!* was not put together intellectually but by the revelation I received from God, on how the Body of Christ should conduct herself so as to maximally partake of the greater glory, which God is pouring out in these last days. Even if you have read this book once, I advise you to read it over and over again, reflect on it and also discuss it with others. The more you do, the more you discover new treasures it contains.

The Christian race is not a sprint but a marathon. Whichever stage you are in right now, please do not be discouraged, but keep pressing on by looking up to Jesus, who will energize you to carry on and finish the race well. To fortify you in the process, there are personalized scriptures on Pages 121-125 based on believer's position in Christ. Endeavor to meditate on it daily so that it can be planted in your heart.

Be on the lookout for the next book in the *Just BE!* Series. Before then, I pray that you continually wax strong, as you look unto Jesus, the author and finisher of our faith.

# *Meditation On Believer's Position In Christ*

*In Christ I am washed, sanctified and I am justified in the Name of my Lord Jesus Christ and by the Spirit of God.*
**1 Corinthians 6:11**

*In Christ I have been buried through baptism into death; that just as Christ was raised from the dead by the glory of the Father, even so I also walk in newness of life.*
**Romans 6:4**

*In Christ I have become the righteousness of God because God has made Jesus who knew no sin to be sin for me.*
**2 Corinthians 5:21**

*In Christ I am chosen before the foundation of the world that I should be holy and without blame before Him in Love.*
**Ephesians 1:4**

*In Christ I am joined together with the church, which as a whole building grows into a holy temple in the Lord.*
**Ephesians 2:21**

*In Christ I have been given the promise of life and righteousness by faith because I believe.*
**Galatians 3:21-22**

*In Christ I know the Holy Scriptures, which are able to make me wise for salvation through faith.*
**2 Timothy 3:15**

*In Christ I have the hope of Christ's coming and I purify myself just as He is pure.*
**1 John 3:2-3**

*In Christ I am dead to the law through the body of Jesus Christ so that I am now in union to Jesus Christ who was raised from the dead and I do now bear fruit to God.*
**Romans 7:4**

*In Christ I am built together for a habitation of God in the Spirit.*
**Ephesians 2:22**

*In Christ I am a new creation; old things have passed away and all things have become new.*
**2 Corinthians 5:17**

*In Christ I am God's workmanship created for good works, which God prepared beforehand that I should walk in them.*
**Ephesians 2:10**

*In Christ I press on, that I may lay hold of that for which Christ Jesus has also laid hold of me. In Christ I press toward the goal for the prize of the upward call of God.*
**Philippians 3:12, 14**

*In Christ I abide in Him and He abides in me for I keep His commandments.*
**1 John 3:24**

*In Christ I, who was once darkness, am now a light in the Lord and I walk as a child of light.*
**Ephesians 5:8**

*In Christ I am filled with the fruits of righteousness to the glory and praise of God.*
**Philippians 1:11**

*In Christ my conscience is purged from dead works by the blood of Jesus Christ so that I do now serve the living God.*
**Hebrews 9:14**

*In Christ I have boldness to enter the Holiest by the blood of Jesus Christ, by a new and living way, which He consecrated for me, through the veil, that is, His flesh.*
**Hebrews 10:19-20**

*In Christ I walk in the light as He is in the light, and I have fellowship with one another and the blood of Jesus Christ cleanses me from all sin.*
**1 John 1:7**

*In Christ I keep God's Word and the love of God is perfected in me.*
**1 John 2:5**

*In Christ I abide in Him and walk just as He walked.*
**1 John 2:6**

*In Christ I abide in Him and he abides in me and I know this because He has given me of His Spirit.*
**1 John 4:13**

*In Christ God has reconciled me to Himself and has given me the ministry of reconciliation.*
**2 Corinthians 5:18**

*In Christ I have access by faith into His grace in which I stand, and rejoice in hope of the glory of God.*
**Romans 5:2**

*In Christ I have been justified by faith, and I have peace with God through my Lord Jesus Christ.*
**Romans 5:1**

*In Christ I am made complete in every good work to do His will through the blood of the everlasting covenant, the blood of Jesus Christ.*
**Hebrews 13:20-21**

*In Christ I have been crucified and it is no longer I who live but Christ who lives in me; and the life, which I now live in the flesh, I live by the faith of the Son of God who loved me and gave Himself for me.*
**Galatians 2:20**

*In Christ I am no longer subjected to the things of this world for I have died with Christ from the basic principles of the world.*
**Colossians 2:20**

*In Christ I live and feed on Him just as Jesus was sent of the Father and lived by the Father.*
**John 6:57**

*In Christ I come to the Father for He is the Way, the Truth and the life.*
**John 14:6**

*In Christ I feed on His words which are spirit and life and He abides in me and I in Him.*
**John 6:56, 63**

*In Christ I know that He is in the Father, and I am in Him and He is in me.*
**John 14:20**

*In Christ I live and move and have my being.*
**Acts 17:28**

*In Christ I bear much fruit for I am a branch in Him and He is the Vine; I abide in Him and He abides in me for without Him I can do nothing.*
**John 15:4-5**

*In Christ I ask what I desire and it is done for me because I abide in Him and His words abide in me. In Christ I am loved in the same manner as the Father loves Jesus and I abide in His love.*
**John 15:7, 9**

*In Christ I do the works of Jesus and greater works because Jesus has gone to the Father and has sent me the Holy Spirit of Truth who abides in me forever.*
**John 14:12, 16, 17**

*In Christ I give thanks to God who gives me the victory through my Lord Jesus Christ.*
**1 Corinthians 15:57**

# A New Life

Ever since the fall of man, sin and death became the nature of every man. Hence, there is the need for man to be regenerated from the inside, in order to be reconnected with God. Jesus literally offered His life to pay the price of the sin of the first man. He sacrificed His life to bring mankind back to His lost glory.

Jesus has done His part by offering Himself as the sacrifice for your sin through His crucifixion. Now you need to do your part by acknowledging what He did for you in His death and resurrection.

Simply put, you need to be born again. For that reason, I encourage you to pray the following prayer in order to receive your salvation:

*Heavenly Father, I come to you as a sinner through Your Son, Jesus Christ who died and rose on the third day and is now seated at Your right hand. I confess all my sins and I invite Jesus into my life as my Lord and Savior. Thank you Jesus because my sins are forgiven. Holy Spirit, I invite you to partner with me in my walk with Jesus. In Jesus name I pray. Amen!*

Congratulations! This is the best decision you have ever made. Please, do not look back! Look for a Bible-believing church where the unadulterated Word of God is taught and preached and begin to attend it regularly.

As soon as you find a Bible believing church, get involved as a new convert so that you can grow spiritually. You can also get in touch with our ministry for resources in your new walk with Jesus.

You will not regret your decision to follow Christ as long as you do not go back to your former ways. May the Lord God bless and sustain you in Jesus' name. I am waiting to hear from you. You can write to me through the address on Page 130.

There is heaven, a glorious place of rest; and hell, a place where torment has no end. Your choice today to give your heart to Christ has secured your spot in heaven as long as you don't turn back.

It is my earnest prayer that God would meet your needs to help you succeed! *Just BE!*

# About The Author

Innovative, wise, creative, funny and loving are some ways Bobby Perry has been acknowledged. He is the founder and pastor of Kingdom Builders' Worship Center, Inc. in Boston, MA. God has deposited in him a mandate to teach the "Kingdom Agenda" through effectual instruction and a passionate lifestyle of worship.

His goal is specific: "establish the Kingdom of God on earth as it is in Heaven" as instructed in Matthew 6:10. The ministry has grown from twenty-five members at its inception, to a congregation of over 1000 "Kingdom Builders."

Built upon a strong, biblically strategic foundation, Kingdom Builders' Worship Center continues to enlarge its territory with a steady increase in fruitful growing "kingdom builders" that boast Bobby Perry as their spiritual leader worldwide. As a worshipper and songwriter, he has produced two albums with his group Bobby Perry and RAIN entitled *All About You* (2006) and *Conquerors* (2011).

Perry desires that all mankind would experience the presence and anointing of God through his ministry.

# Contact Information

We want to hear from you. Please send your comments about this book to us in care of the address below. Thank you.

Bishop Bobby Perry
Kingdom Builders Worship Center
234 Norfolk Street
Boston
Massachusetts 02124
USA

Phone: 617-474-9871
Email: **bishopperry@gmail.com**
Twitter: **twitter.com/iambobbyperry**
Facebook: **facebook.com/iambobbyperry**
Website: **www.bobbyperryonline.com**
**www.thekingdomchurch.com**

You can order additional copies of this book @

www.amazon.com
www.barnesandnoble.com
www.bobbyperryonline.com

or by mail through the postal address above.

# Other Products By The Ministry

## All About You

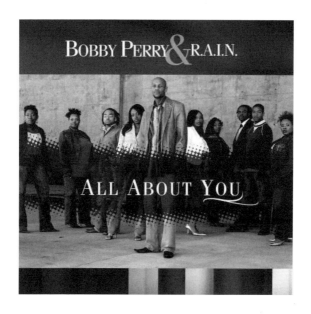

*All About You*, the debut summer release 2006 by Bobby Perry & RAIN (Royal Agents Influencing Nations) arrives just in time to shake up a genre that is quickly becoming repetitive. Featuring eleven tracks of tight R&B, hip hop and contemporary soul beats, superior vocal harmonies and phrasings, all built around Christ centered lyrics, *All About You* immediately thrusts Bobby Perry and RAIN to the forefront of Urban Gospel.

# Conquerors

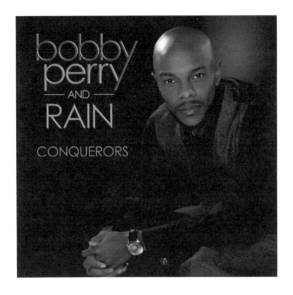

The incomparable Bobby Perry and RAIN (Royal Agents Influencing Nations) returns with his much-anticipated sophomore album on Solaria Records entitled *Conquerors*. This creative masterpiece resurrects deep and spiritually enriching foundations of traditional gospel songwriting allied with highly energetic and astutely interpreted urban gospel arrangements. The eleven tracks on *Conquerors* feature tight R&B, hip hop, middle eastern, classical and contemporary soul arrangements intertwined with superior vocal harmonies and phrasing, all built around Christ centered lyrics. Bobby takes us on a journey that not only invokes the genius of old, but also unifies us across cultures both in lyric and in instrumentation. From deeply contemplative tracks that will heal broken hearts to truck thumping bangers that will literally move the heart, *Conquerors* is sure to be the long awaited reintroduction of one of Gospel's finest sons.